GIVE YOURSELF PERMISSION TO BE STRONG

GIVE YOURSELF PERMISSION TO BE VULNERABLE

GIVE YOURSELF PERMISSION TO BE RIGHT

GIVE YOURSELF PERMISSION TO BE WRONG

GIVE YOURSELF PERMISSION TO FOLLOW THROUGH
ON WHAT FRIGHTENS YOU MOST

GIVE YOURSELF PERMISSION TO LET GO OF PAST HURT

GIVE YOURSELF PERMISSION TO RELEASE TOXIC PEOPLE

GIVE YOURSELF PERMISSION TO SPEAK UP AND BE HEARD

GIVE YOURSELF PERMISSION TO NOT GO ALONG WITH THE GO-ALONG

GIVE YOURSELF PERMISSION TO GO AGAINST THE GRAIN

GIVE YOURSELF PERMISSION TO STOP NEEDING APPROVAL

GIVE YOURSELF PERMISSION TO BE EXTRAORDINARY, WITHOUT APOLOGY

GIVE YOURSELF PERMISSION TO BE BEYOND ENOUGH

BEYOND ENOUGH
How to Lead with Your Whole Self

Raquel Eatmon

Rising Media LLC ~ USA

To every seven-year-old girl with a dream,
every girl that will someday be seven,
and every girl who was once seven.

CONTENTS

Acknowledgments

My life is greatly enhanced because of the people in my inner circle. From the moment I decided to write Beyond Enough a spiritual concourse of magnificent people with heartfelt intentions showed up for this project and they have enormously supported my work, my research and my dreams.

Thank you Cheri Phyfer for your encouraging and heartwarming words in the foreword. Thank you Colleen Durgarte and Diana Bilimoria for lending your voice to Beyond Enough. I appreciate your support, love and well wishes. I extend an enormous amount of gratitude to Susan Baracco, the story architect for women, who motivated me to tell my story and helped paved a crystal clear road to express it and share with others. Thank you Michael LaRocca for the final edit.

To my dear, sweet, loving friends who have rallied around every single word, Jana K, Marsha and Roxanne, thank you for being my sheroes. Your accountability calls and feedback have kept me on my toes and in check with the universal order of getting it all done.

More girl magic has surrounded Beyond Enough with my graphic designer Dana Anderson whose creative insight helped bring my intention, passion and purpose into one cohesive message.

This book would not be possible without the many women and men who have supported my work in women's empowerment through my leadership forums. These people have infused my work with passion, all of which brings me great joy. Thank you: Bob Klonk, Ken Lanci, Trina Evans, Karen Harper, Elizabeth Brooks and Diane Smith. Thank you again Colleen D. for your fresh perspective, you've made the ride outrageously fun.

And to my colleagues, acquaintances and business associates, I am elated to share this project with each of you.

Mostly, however, I want to acknowledge a small group of people who are very much a big part of my life. To my dear mother Kay, thank you for holding my hand on that first day of school and for continuing to hold it today. You are a treasure. I'm glad we have traveled this journey together. To my step-father Terry, thank you for standing up for me when the rest of the world fell silent. Your support changed my life. To Roy, thank you for your support and sincere support over all of the years. They have made an impact. To Markietta, the laughs and routine check-ins taught me that this is what spiritual sisters do. Thank you for showing me a sisterhood without judgment.

Finally, to my wonderful, adoring husband Dexter who has witnessed my personal journey to Enoughness, your lovingness has taught me how to fly and how to love. Je t'aime.

FOREWORD

You have probably heard or used the phrase "actions speak louder than words." Raquel has finally taken her actions and put them into words to help other women achieve success in their career journeys. Empowering women to be the best versions of themselves has been Raquel's mission for the last decade. She travels the country speaking on critical women's topics, has successfully pioneered an impactful annual women's leadership conference, launched a blog, and now authored this insightful self-discovery book for women.

As leaders we share a like-mindedness to help others and to help build the communities we serve. I have witnessed Raquel's strong commitment to impact women through her social change initiative. In 2017 Raquel acted on her relentless desire to bring one of Time Magazine's Most Influential People in the World, Sister Rosemary Nyirumbe, to Cleveland from Gulu, Uganda.

It was a bold step but Raquel believed that the Sister's story of helping human trafficking survivors was relevant to Ohioans. The statistic hit close to home. I, along with a small team of women, worked with Raquel to develop content and build a platform for Sister Rosemary's message. The diverse audience was made up of a mixture of women from young college students to Baby Boomers. It was a surreal experience to join in the discussion and learn more about playing a role in positively impacting the workplace and community.

While the world is constantly evolving, overcoming the challenges of being a woman in the working world continues to be a significant issue. This book is a must-have resource for women who are seeking opportunities to lead authentically. Finding your authentic leadership style is what will set you apart as a female leader. The best advice I was given as a young leader was don't try to be like anyone else. Be yourself.

Raquel breaks down the issues we face as women. She organizes them into meaningful and digestible sections, finishing each with a tip or life tool that helps you take action and find your true self. Reading and acting on this book will build your confidence, your awareness and your ability to lead others.

This book is for every woman. Reading it is like getting a pep talk and a hug from a close friend. Raquel has an ability to make it real through her personal stories. She gives you a peek inside her world as a child, teenager and mature woman. And I have no doubt you will see yourself in many places. This book has the potential to change your life if you let it.

Cheri Phyfer
President
Moen U.S. Businesses

An unravel, we must do.

WHY YOU SHOULD LISTEN TO ME

Sounds like a gutsy enough move, doesn't it? Starting a book with a bold statement. But it is a question I had to ponder while writing this book. After all, there are between 600,000 and 1,000,000 books published each year, both on paper and electronically, and this may be the one to tip over the entire shelf or fill the storage in your app. Would it be just another thing for you to read? And another great question authors confront is 'who cares?' What's in it for you, the reader?

I'm not a celebrity on a big screen or a housewife with continual · drama unfolding. Pop culture has not tagged me as the "It Girl" or "Most Pouty Lips." My life hasn't played out on an international stage. The bumps, bruises and wins have been personal and obscure. But it has happened nonetheless. The obscurity doesn't negate my story, my lessons or my passion to share my truth and my hopes to save others from an unhappy, unfulfilled existence.

So back to this gutsy thing. Yes, I have guts and it's taken time to not only admit to having them but to say it out loud without apprehension. It's taken time to own it. Like the laugh lines on my face, I've earned that gutsiness. I am proud of that.

So, celebrity I am not but I am a fan of living a big life. Transparency is part of living a big life. Life is easier when I'm transparent. My relationships work better, and my business thrives. I sleep better which makes me happy. Being transparent also allows us to pinpoint our worth.

Transparency bolsters self-worth. To get there, we must gather up the pieces we have lost along the way. Those are the same pieces that cause us to question ourselves and second guess things. The same pieces that promote insecurity and leave us questioning: Am I enough?

You are beyond enough.

Even if you stumbled once, twice or 112 times, you are enough. You will lose your way or feel insignificant, but it can all work towards a greater good. No hard lesson or embarrassing situation goes unused.

All of these experiences add incredible value to our lives if we allow them to. Most of us, however, get caught up in the words and meanings of mistakes and regrets. We beat ourselves up more than anyone else does. But there is another option. We can move into a different realm that is limitless and powerful.

There are some life situations that you have absolutely no control over. You can't choose your family or birthplace. A few things are predetermined. And out of millions and millions of decisions, experiences and choices, only a few are already made for us. We have more power over our lives than we know or believe. I believe in owning this power. I want you to own your power.

I wrote Beyond Enough in celebration of who we are. Who. We. Are. Right. Now. The woman who shows up each day with fatigue and confusion. The brave and resilient SHE-ro who carries everyone on her back. The lady who is just getting by and doesn't want to bother anyone for anything. The storyteller. The challenger. The aggressor. The doormat. The fearful one. The strong one. The angry one. The loving one. The one. You.

After hitting personal and professional bottom and struggling for insight, and a way out of the mayhem, I promised myself that I would spread the word to prevent another woman from falling into that pit. I've been there. You don't want to go there and you don't have to.

You don't have to run from ambition or a call to step up and claim your seat at the table. You don't have to be ashamed of wanting to achieve big goals or thinking outside of the norm.

Each of us at this very moment has the capacity to take our lives to an extraordinary level by accepting our Enoughness. Becoming one with our Enoughness does more than empower self, it empowers everyone in our circle. It affects the entire world. It is contagious and exquisite. Exposing our Enoughness puts us in a space of grace and magnificence. Yes, it's that good. It is freeing.

I now know this freedom well because there was a time when I was stuck in chaos. My life sent glaring alarms and I ignored them. I wrote them off as insignificant. I conveniently excused them. I was fixated on how life was supposed to be rather than what it actually was. Transparency felt oceans away.

When life has something to tell you, it doesn't stop because you are in denial. It keeps coming back, stronger, harder and louder until it grabs your attention.

Before I started my company, I worked as a television news reporter and anchor. My desire to highlight issues plaguing disenfranchised people inspired me to take this road. Over time I became frustrated with the business. The sensationalism halted my groove. I was disenchanted with the "If it bleeds, it leads" mantra, which really is the nature of the "beast," but it wasn't in my nature. Many times my pitch to tell stories of relevance fell on deaf ears.

My biggest challenge was from a self-proclaimed perfectionist manager. He called me during commercials while I was on the news desk and questioned my choice of lipstick color. He demanded that I be consistent with my hairstyle, pointing to the polished look plastered on billboards around the city. He also questioned my diction, how I pronounced "the" and "a."

On top of that, an angry viewer sent death threats. "Mmm, let's see," I thought. "I'm telling viewers the worst thing that happened in their world today, getting blasted over lipstick and dealing with an unstable viewer. Is this job worth it?"

Honestly, the bigger question I had to ask is "Am I worth more than this?"

Bingo! That was the question I needed to ask to reframe my reality of who I was and what I meant to myself. Not to flaky bosses, crazy viewers, or anyone else. To me.

I walked away from it all. The large salary. The big billboards. The small-minded manager. All of it. Raquel has left the building. Unsure of my next move, I needed to find my way back to wholeness. I took time to heal.

But healing was nowhere in sight. Instead, a recession rolled in, taking my savings and most of my possessions with it. My husband's work was cut in half, so we went through our savings and dipped into the 401K accounts. We had to downsize and move into an efficiency apartment. We sold my paid-for dream car, a black-on-black Mercedes S420, because we couldn't afford the upkeep. It was difficult to part with that car because I worked hard for my money. I wanted to enjoy some of what I earned. With each paycheck, I had stashed money into my bank account, preparing for this car.

I'll never forget the first test drive; I was smiling ear to ear. I jumped on the highway and the ride was as smooth as a sailboat on still water. What I loved most about the car was how safe I felt while driving it. The body of the car was heavy and you could feel it when you pressed on the gas. It was a big difference from the other old clunkers I owned that typically had more rust than paint.

My Mercedes wasn't the only thing to go because we couldn't afford the upkeep. The hair, nails and facials were a thing of the past. It was an odd spiral. Yes, things hit bottom but it all seemed so purposeful. I was being stripped down, turned around and redirected.

From the vantage point of that drought, I peered inside myself. It takes guts to look at the unflattering side of yourself when life chews you up and spits you out but this is where the truly valuable, authentic gems are. I began to see that I was enough. Me, Raquel - I was more than enough without all the other stuff.

I got busy. I developed the Woman of Power Conference (WoPC) and built a forum for transparent leadership. It started in a small hotel in Bellville, Ohio and it has grown to be the premier conference in the Midwest, attracting partnerships with companies such as KeyBank, Vitamix, Sherwin Williams and others.

WoPC wasn't just a platform for other women, it was for me too. I was feeling some disconnects, some uncertainty. I was still healing, while my voice was recharging.

I dove into my work. Researching and studying every day. I made it my mantra to tell myself the truth. If I was going to go all in for myself, then I needed to wrap around a cool-to-the-touch bottle of truth serum.

This wasn't about me lying to myself. It was about staying clear of the untruths society and pop culture (and that boss) had thrown my way. It was about interrupting and eventually ending the voices in my head of the manager and all the others who had a negative influence in my life.

Once I gained clarity, my worth was obvious. It was bold and impressive. It was loud and significant. It rocked and stilled me at the same time. That is when I understood fully and completely that I am more than enough, just as I am. You are too.

However, discovering your truth and knowing your worth isn't enough. Having all the tools in the world isn't enough if you don't know how to use them. It's like owning a shiny new corporate jet waiting to take you wherever you want to go but you have no clue how to find a pilot or even start it, or make it take you anywhere. It's useless.

The best tools in the world are useless if you don't know how to use them or worse, you choose to not use them at all.

We are enough in the ruins and we are enough in the tides. Believing this takes time, knowing this takes courage, and being this requires a definitive choice.

If I could write a letter to my younger self, this book would be it. If I could give a gift to every single woman in the world, this book would be it. This is a love letter addressed to each of you and to myself. It is a personal confession of my love and admiration to women around the world to step boldly and fully into their Enoughness without question.

Regardless of the hand we've been dealt, understanding our complete worth is paramount. I was raised by three women whom you will read about later, and I learned that if you didn't value yourself, you didn't value anything.

Beyond Enough is about owning every aspect of your life, your person and your results.

You will read about three essential parts: Worth, Wisdom and Wholeness. There are nuggets of insight layered on each page. This book is formatted for you to read cover to cover or to leaf through it and savor a section that is pertinent to you today. Take your time. There are no rules. Take what you need.

Thank you for rolling with me.
Raquel

BEYOND ENOUGH
How to Lead with Your Whole Self

Raquel Eatmon

What if the gems beneath
the rhetoric are already
perfectly polished?

What if you allowed that
glow to swell up through
you, without questions,
apologies or pause?

PART ONE: BE WORTHY

I choose me.

Saying those words is not easy for most people. In fact, taking that step is nearly impossible for many. Getting there has taken me many hikes through upset, confusion and fear, all of which stripped away parts of my worthiness and healthy self-esteem. These breakdowns interfere with the honor we want to hold true for ourselves. They are the most indecent of proposals, loaded with trade-offs of suffering and shamefulness. Losing the ability to stand firmly in our worth is a lonely, terrifying way to live.

I didn't always choose me. In fact, I once wrote a letter to a group of the popular girls in junior high school telling them why they should let me join their group. At the end of the letter, I drew two boxes: Check yes or no. I nervously gave the letter to the captain of the group. She was blonde and always had sticky hands. An impossibly long two days later, without any interaction, the captain peeled that folded paper from her hand and gave it to me. She turned quickly and walked away, her plaid jumper twisting enough to hinder her progress. They didn't choose me. I was hurt. Not stunned, but definitely hurt.

Kids do and say strange things but you don't realize that as a kid. I wanted to ask them why they foolishly checked "No" (with a big red thick-tip marker, mind you) but instead I wondered what made them so popular anyway and what was wrong with me. I wanted to know who gave them the right to reject me!?! As a girl, growing up in a family that was mixed with love, pain and destructive behaviors, my models of self worth were not the best. They had their issues, and their issues became my issues. Asking them about this sort of thing didn't feel like the right thing to do.

START A LOVE AFFAIR

Feeling a sense of worthlessness from the girl with the twisted plaid jumper and her cronies was just a small sample of the rejection and big red "no's" coming my way. More piled on. People didn't always choose me. During my adolescent years through college, I was getting tired of sending the proverbial notes of acceptance. I was beginning to understand the surest way to be chosen was to choose myself.

That was the beginning of a unique love affair with myself, not the arrogant kind but the healing kind. I began sending love to my three-year-old self straight through to my very grown self today. It is part of my honor code. I accept all of me. I have nurtured the spirit of my younger self and healed wounds. By using the techniques and principles that I share with you in these pages, and doing the work, I began a long love affair with my one-day-old self, my 13-year-old self, all the way up to this very moment. Sure, there are hiccups and setbacks, but they are easily managed, they are not a hindrance.

Choosing yourself after everything you have been through is a no small feat. You have to hurdle over those power-draining experiences. But once you choose you, the reward points continue accumulating without an expiration date. When you get centered in your Enoughness, you refuel your worthiness and generate an emotional bloom that never wilts.

THE EFFECTS OF AFTERBURN

Long before making waves in the TV news broadcasting business, I was a fitness instructor. Unfortunately, I allowed my certification to expire along with my abs, but many of the elements of physical fitness are still part of my life. Today, the industry has a term, EPOC, which is an acronym for Exercise Post Oxygen Consumption, which some people refer to as afterburn. Essentially, EPOC is the amount of oxygen required to restore your body to its normal, resting level of metabolic function. Because the workout is so tough, you require more oxygen after the strenuous exercise session, and while the body settles back into its normal zone you continue to need more oxygen. I compare it to taking a long trip in your car: After you reach your destination, your engine doesn't automatically cool, it is a gradual cool down after all of that exertion. After a workout, your body does the same thing. What fitness folks love about this is that EPOC helps our bodies continue burning calories after the heavy lifting is done. The workout is done but the burn keeps burning.

Choosing yourself now will reap lasting results long after you do the work. I am talking about forgoing excuses and current behaviors and putting in the long-term hard effort that will last.

Putting the pedal to the metal now inspires change like nothing else in your life.

Worth is not measured by anything physical, it is all on the inside. It is what you put into it. People on the outside can't see it. They only see the physical package Getting established in your Enoughness requires you to trust in what you cannot see. Trust it. Do your absolute best. Put it all on the line. Have hope. Have grit.

There are many components to self-worth. A lot comes into play here. As you prepare to dive into this section, picture in your mind a small, smart-looking piece of roller luggage that we will call your Enoughness Bag. Go ahead, picture a Gucci or Vuitton or a slick black leather bag with your own personal logo. What goes in it? Beautiful tools of Enoughness. Throughout this section, I will show you some of the most beautiful tools of Enoughness to put in your bag. Each one of the following sections serves a purpose in building your value and worth. Once you have them, they're yours forever. No one can take them away.

Integrity is doing what you said you would do, when you said you would do it, and when you fall short, you clean it up. Repeat.

INTEGRITY

Leading a dishonorable life encourages chaos. We attract troublesome relationships and we struggle and suffer within. If we can't tell ourselves the truth and accept it, we have no integrity. If you don't have integrity you cannot be honorable to others, so you cannot possibly lead an honorable life. It's a falsehood that we can have one without the other. We are lying to ourselves if this is our belief.

You are sure to recognize the traits of a person with integrity. One is doing what you said you would do when you said you would do it. It is being a woman of your word. Integrity is a big responsibility because you have to show up. Showing up only some of the time means promises are broken, we renege on our word. Sometimes life happens, some things throw us off course, and we might let others down along the way. But as my grandmother would say, "One monkey don't stop no show." In other words, one letdown or dishonoring your word doesn't mean your moral character is in question. You simply need to clean it up and reassure yourself and others involved that you are back on the right course.

Another trait of living a life of integrity is doing the right thing when no one is looking. Many people are on display, seeking attention and doing good things to attract a crowd. But who are they when the lights are out? Who are they when the rest of the world is busy looking in the other direction?

One cold, winter afternoon I was visiting a television news station near downtown Cleveland. As I waited for my appointment, I looked through the window. The street was busy with traffic and a few bundled-up pedestrians. I noticed a familiar face walking down the street. It was one of the investigative reporters, Adam. I watched him walk toward the crosswalk only to stop, turn around, back up, and pick up a couple pieces of litter from the sidewalk. He tossed them into a trash can and continued on his way.

It wasn't his trash but it was his choice. He chose to tidy up a space he shared with the public. I don't know the reasoning behind his choice, but this small act said something about Adam. It told me something about his values and his ability to be the same person in the spotlight as well as when no one was looking. He had no idea that I or anyone else in that building was watching him through the dark windows.

MAKE IT RIGHT

When you see something wrong, try to make it right. It can be as simple as sprucing up your community. Becoming a woman of your word can be easily achieved by choosing to do the right thing, over and over again. When you misstep, clean it up. We all have the ability to restore our integrity.

You owe it to yourself to be rooted in the value-based principle of integrity because it benefits everyone in your life, especially yourself. When you own the truth, you are moving to a higher level of self-awareness. When you own it, you are swimming in your Enoughness.

When Michelle Obama spoke to millions of Americans during the 2008 Democratic Convention, she shared several personal stories about her childhood growing up in Chicago. She told the audience that she was raised with an important value, "Your word is your bond and you do what you say you're going to do; that you treat people with dignity and respect." Integrity was a value ingrained in Mrs. Obama during her formative years.

It is wonderful to have this structure so early in life but many people pick up the pieces much later. Or if we get them early on, we might lose them, become unhinged and need redirecting. You will find that when you get them doesn't matter. What matters is what you do with it when an opportunity crosses your path. Having honor, respect and dignity is the definition of a rich life. These traits can do a lot more than elevate an impoverished mind and hurting soul. They can also add a bling to a highly skilled professional.

START PACKING!

As you pack the Be Worthy compartment of your Enoughness Bag, it is up to you how to organize it, but you should always pack it with an emergency in mind. You want to fill it with the things that you need for the journey, keeping your most critical items close by. Just like before the takeoff of a flight, when the attendant asks you to store your luggage in the overhead, keeping a few essential things within reach, you will want to have your most critical tools where you can easily access them in case of an emergency. These are the things you can't live without.

The same action is needed with the Self Worth compartment; you'll want the must-have items within arm's reach all of the time. Your integrity is one of those items.

ENOUGHNESS TOOL #1: ASSESS YOUR INTEGRITY

These five questions can change your life right now. Use these questions as a self-check guide for gauging your level of integrity:

1. Am I the same person when I'm in the spotlight that I am when I'm alone?
2. How well do I treat people from whom I can gain nothing?
3. When I have something to say about people, do I talk to them or about them?
4. Do I have an unchanging standard for moral decisions, or do circumstances determine my choices?
5. Do I quickly admit wrongdoing without being pressed to do so?

This is a short list so feel free to add to it when you are ready. You might start with one question a day or focus on one each week. However you choose to work the list, be prepared for new insight. Be prepared to find tremendous value within.

*Stop anticipating the outcome; start searching
for what you can not yet see.*

POSSIBILITIES

What if? It is a powerful question on its own. It is quite easy to get caught up in asking the traditional questions we were taught during our formative years: Who, What, When, Where, Why and How? What our teachers didn't know or think to share is how limiting this so-called starting lineup can be. Those questions keep our brains thinking about outcome. We are fixated on the result, which inhibits our thinking and seeing beyond the experience. We are wrapped up in the totality of what is happening, unable to imagine beyond it.

We want to live a life of great meaning. We want to master happiness and feel loved and appreciated. All of us want success and gratification. But the trek toward accomplishment always feels like an uphill battle.

Are we always going to be fighting for something or someone?

That was the question that changed my outlook on what I call the corporate shuffle, or the entrepreneurial hustle. I pondered: how much harder can it get and why is it so hard anyway? Those questions didn't inspire change. Instead, they attracted more challenges. I stopped anticipating outcomes and started searching for what I could not yet see. The vision that I, the girl from a small Midwest town and a struggling family, could not yet fathom.

LIMITING BELIEFS

Before landing a job in TV news I held a few different jobs. One was at a cosmetic counter in a department store and shortly thereafter a community news reporter for a non-profit. In each of those jobs, people around me were being promoted. That told me two things: first, there wasn't a lack of opportunity and second, there was something lacking in me.

As I worked to polish my skills I worked equally hard to eliminate negative thoughts about the tough journey ahead. I grew up in a tough environment so my paradigm was about the glass always being half empty. I had to rewire some things. So I began to monitor my self-talk. When that didn't seem to work, I asked myself, "How do you know the outcome of the race, you're not even fully on the track?"

I was living under the weight of many limiting beliefs. Beliefs like there isn't enough for everyone and money doesn't grow on trees (that was always a confusing one to me because paper is made from trees so money does sort of grow on trees).

I settled on this one point: How do I know, how can I know the outcome of any of it? No one knows and since I don't know, I might be able to persuade things to flow my way. Since I don't yet know the result, anything is possible.

This new line of thinking introduced me to new people. I received invites to events I had only dreamed of attending. And I landed my very first TV news job. Years prior, I worked tirelessly to get into the TV business and was rejected at least two dozen times. I wholeheartedly believe that when I delved into the realm of possibility, it changed my approach and my ability to let go and stop being so rigid with expectations. It was effortless. A friend called a friend, I auditioned and the job was mine. That's it.

DIFFERENT THINKING EQUALS POSSIBILITIES

I experienced so much joy from the results of my actions. One of those joys was meeting and interviewing my idol: poet, civil rights activist, and author Dr. Maya Angelou. I read her book, I Know Why the Caged Bird Sings, during my teen years. Her words uplifted me. I promised myself I'd meet her. I promised myself she would autograph that same book someday.

Years later, when I discovered that she was scheduled to appear at the University of North Texas for a keynote presentation, I called her team and requested an interview. They asked me to draft a letter, explaining why I wanted to interview Maya. I wrote my heart out. At the time, the producers at my station didn't have an interest in such a story, there was nothing to sensationalize, but I was interested in Maya's voice resonating through the airwaves to my female audience, I knew she could make an impact.

Because this wasn't a tabloid-ish story, because Maya walked the straight and narrow, my news team wasn't interested. I wasn't going to be paid for the work and I wouldn't have access to any of the station's resources: Camera operator, lights, etc. There was no way in hell I was going to forego this opportunity over short-sighted people. I switched my schedule with another reporter, paid one of our news photographers to shoot it, and out to UNT we went. The moment I saw Dr. Angelou walk through the door, I reached into my pocket and touched that old book and I couldn't help but tear up. I was overwhelmed with emotion because I knew this meeting would someday happen. I didn't have all of the particulars—when, how, or why—but none of that mattered. I knew it would happen.

LETTING GO

Relinquishing my attachment to results and outcomes was a turning point. Understanding and accepting what I think I know is limiting. What if the result is bigger than you expect? What if the result brings new people and ideas and financing to the table? What if? I had to be willing to take a gamble on these questions, After all, other than complaints, I didn't have much to lose.

What would your life look like if you could focus your attention on executing tasks and building your skill set instead of contemplating the outcome of your work? What if you could be the absolute best version of yourself and build exceptional relationships without worry or fear?

This is what living in the realm of possibility looks like. There are no limits. When you choose to live this way, you are essentially choosing to be courageous. People who explore possibilities are mentally tough too. They are disciplined self-starters. They manage their thoughts and emotions. They view problems as wise teachers because when you learn, you grow. Limitless thinkers are the epitome of optimists. Coloring outside of the lines isn't available to only a select group. You can do this too. Here are a few tips to get it going:

ENOUGHNESS TOOL #2: EMBRACE YOUR POWER
1. Put it All on the Table: Imagine how fierce you would be if you stepped up to exploring possibilities and giving yourself permission to dream and play. Step up to your next big thing...every day. Do your best, put forth your best effort, enjoy the process and let the outcome take care of itself. To live fully you have to remove the limits. Discard the dead weight and replace it with action, massive action. Move in any direction you want. Move quickly. Upgrade the wheels on your Enoughness bag from the traditional ones to the sleek, fast spinner wheels to really charge at a new pace.

2. Invent New Ways of Being: Consider seeking more positive outcomes and being proactive right now. Contemplate ways to pour into your Enoughness and fill it to the rim. Draft a plan on how you can expose yourself to more successful experiences. This may involve going on a new adventure or being the first to arrive at an event or stepping all the way out of your comfort zone with a new group.

3. Role Model Behavior: Envision someone you admire, someone who appears to be living in a world without limits. Study their behavior and language. Pull some of their charm your way. You don't have to invent anything new here. Everything you need has already arrived. You just have to go for it.

*Cop-outs will hold you hostage, blocking you
from extraordinary success.
They inhibit our ability to positively influence others
and live authentically.*

RESPONSIBLE LIVING

Excuses take energy, depleting it quickly. Not only do you need to invent the excuse, but you also need to assign blame. Then you put up a guard. All this effort drains you spiritually and emotionally. We're waiting on and wading in excuses. They keep us shallow which robs us of being enough and having enough.

People hide behind excuses. It's a cowardly place to live. We hide not only in our professional lives but in our personal lives as well. How many times have you said, "I'll start my new eating program on Monday" or "I'm going to make the changes New Year's Day!" or "I'll call him next week when I can find the right words to say." I used those and other excuses at a time in my life.

My dear high school track coach, Wilbur Lanier, wouldn't accept any excuses from me or my classmates. We were as slick as they come but Coach Lanier had our number and never hesitated to call us out. His stern and straightforward demeanor had a great impact on me.

When we made excuses for losing a race or being late for practice, he'd yell, "Excuses are like a-holes, everyone has one, get things done! Regardless!"

We listened. He made us into better runners and more accountable human beings. Under his leadership I released the need to make excuses for my shortcomings and began hitting goals that seemed too big at the time. Coach's lessons taught me that I was responsible for pulling the plug on my own success.

MORE AFTERBURN

Although Coach Lanier had a deep baritone voice, he wasn't a huge talker. He was about action. His coaching technique was different from any coach or teacher in our district. His instructions didn't always resonate during practice, but many of his applications hit home during real life experiences. He pushed us to be better people and he pushed us to run hard. It seemed that each time my mind swayed from the race, he was there to forcefully get me back on track.

This was also the case at an away track meet in a small Ohio town just under an hour's drive from home. I was 15 years old and it was always exciting to be out of town, seeing new people (boys) and competing against new runners (in that order). Before the meet began, I stopped by the concession stand and a super cool boy stood next to me and started flirting. As much as I wanted to cave, a surge of fear rushed over me. I was terrified that Coach would walk up and see this gray-eyed stud gazing into my eyes and yank me right out of my spikes. I tried to walk away but this kid grabbed my arm and asked for my phone number. Right on the edge of spilling out the digits, I hear, "Eatmon! You didn't come here to meet knuckleheads, you came here to kick ass, get on that track!"

Coach was standing at the top of the bleachers peering down at me and that sweet boy who was now terrified. Humiliated, I zipped away. I took the long way to Coach's seat. I apologized and told him how the boy approached me, I had nothing to do with it, "You're wasting time," he said. "The amount of energy you're using talkin' about that knucklehead, you could use it on the track, go get things done Eatmon! Just get it done. Regardless!"

Later that evening, after I'd won first place in my solo and relay events, we returned to our school, where our parents were waiting to pick us up. I ran and told my mother about how Coach embarrassed me as he stood nearby listening. My mom looked at me and then over to Coach Lanier. "Thank you," she said. Coached nodded his head and pretended to tip the bill of his ball cap.

Each practice and each track meet, I worked on technique and focus. I wanted to be a better runner. I wanted to explore what would happen if I perfected my races.

After that track season Coach awarded me with a Team Captain plaque and spoke of my leadership and effort to work hard. I was sold on his leadership, even his occasional tossing of the rocks when we hard-headed kids couldn't follow instructions.

GET OUT OF JAIL FREE

There is another type of excuse we've fallen prey to, the excuses that we actually believe or the ones that keep circulating through society like a hall pass or a get out of jail free card. Some of these are now acceptable social behavior. These two examples are most common:

Example 1 - I Gave It My All: Did you really give it your everything? Did you really put it all on the line, every single ounce? Chances are the answer is no. We rarely give something 100% effort. Most people give just enough to scoot by. A lot of folks don't have any idea what 100% looks like yet they'll boast about over-producing.

Stop saying you gave it your all when you didn't. A better approach is to simply say, "I gave it 45.8%" and sit with that number, marinate with that truth. When we become that morally sound with ourselves, our stuff begins to bubble up. We realize how we've been pulling the curtain on our power and how small we have played. We realize how dry and empty the Be Worthy compartment is in our bag. Connecting these behaviors unleashes a newfound testimony of a greater force within you. If you have given your all on a task or relationship, you will walk away knowing that indeed you gave it every single thing you had, therefore you have no regrets.

Example 2 - People Do The Best They Can: No, a lot of them don't do the best they can. In this day and age we have access to an abundance of resources. Nearly every single question you have can be answered in a second through search engines or a voice-activated speaker in your home. I have listened to some people complain about how they can't have a good life or they don't know what steps to take to end a bad relationship. I ask them what steps they took to rectify the problem. Did you Google how to have a good life? Did you Google how to get out of this situation? I'm not suggesting that Google has the magic touch but when people complain about not having the money or skills to get what they want, it makes me wonder how much effort they put forth.

TAKE IT INTO YOUR OWN HANDS

We are capable of taking action to solve our problems. We must stop waiting for others to save us. Googling a work or personal crisis is the first step. This is called being self-sufficient. The next step? Google will likely lead you to a list of books and articles on the subject. Browse the selection, then buy a book or check it out at the library. This is called investing in personal development. Get out there and put your new techniques and tips into action. Practice on people. This is called polishing a skill. Once you study up on the subject and build practical skills, you have a strategy to combat some of life's heavier moments.

The notion that people do the best they can do is a pacifying concept. If folks know how to buy stuff from Amazon and use a can opener (not necessarily at the same time), they know how to search for solutions.

You can probably spot dozens of other statements that excuse us from aiming high. We, as a society, have made it very convenient to play a game of smoke and mirrors with ourselves. It makes us feel better when there is a reason for our failures. When we can explain away the unpleasantries of losing or being rejected it doesn't sting as much.

I believe when you search for the reason behind the excuses, you discover an easier pathway to success. It takes work to unravel old feelings and old stories, but you can get to the source of the issue. Here's how:

ENOUGHNESS TOOL #3: ELIMINATE EXCUSES

1. Evaluate the Source of Excuses: Where does this need originate for you? The need to gloss over a truth with an alibi doesn't just happen, it has a root cause supporting it. Dig deep for answers. It could be connected to a very innocent action from your past. Perhaps you misinterpreted it or accepted it as an imperfection.

2. Commit to Doing the Work: Commit to understanding how excuses are holding you in a space where you don't want to be. Understand that excuses are emotional blocks. They prevent us from making wiser choices. They are crippling even if it appears that you're getting away with something.

3. Reject Temptation: Refuse to give in to old feelings or stories that have power over you. Don't allow old worn-out energy to dictate your future. It is counterproductive and steals your self-worth. Be aware and recognize when negative feelings surface. This will help you conquer them. Instead of making the choice to feel the negativity, make a better choice to evaluate it.

*"Our deepest fear is not that we are inadequate.
Our deepest fear is that we are powerful beyond measure.
It is our light, not our darkness, that most frightens us."*
—Marianne Williamson

FEAR AND ACCOUNTABILITY

We fear letting go, we fear letting people in, we fear getting the job or not getting the job, we fear going to meetings, we fear our talents and hidden potential, we fear not giving it our all, we fear what people will think, we fear letting others down, we fear not being acknowledged, we fear sending that email, we fear asking for what we want, we fear writing the book, we fear being lonely, we fear asking for help, we fear letting go of our our old selves, we fear getting older, we fear change, we fear fear, we fear dying, we fear living.

And so, we are consumed by fear.

This is the reality we bought into and it is robbing us of a quality life. The thievery slithers down, swallowing just about every lifeline we have. We lose out on being loved and giving love. Another big score on this losing team is we never reach our full potential. We never quite meet the *it* girl living within each one of us. We refrain from letting her loose. We refuse to let her run wild with her Enoughness.

DON'T GET THE PITY PARTY STARTED

I will never forget the moment I had a face-to-face meeting with fear. I was stuck and on the brink of a great opportunity. I was questioning everything and I was somehow managing to talk myself out of it through a pity party. I sold myself a story about things falling short. I convinced myself that I was OK with the end result, it was probably better that it didn't work out, and on and on I went. I carried this thought process into a three-day leadership development forum in Columbus, Ohio.

There I was, neatly dressed with manicured nails, perfect make-up and a sewage of thoughts in my head. I sat among 300+ people. We listened to Linda, the facilitator, and she was good. She was damn good. Before I knew it I was at the audience microphone asking a question. I don't recall making a decision to ask a question and I don't recall the question but I remember what happened next.

Linda asked me a few questions about the job opportunity I was entertaining. I responded with all the things that were wrong about it and how a few things didn't align with my values. The audience backed me up with "Oh, now that's not right," and "I wouldn't go for that either." I had an audience, which felt reassuring. Linda told them all to "Stop it!"

"That's the nature of the beast in the business Raquel is in, just stop it," Linda said as she pushed herself out of the director-style chair and left the stage. My eyes followed her. I pondered where she was going. I was disappointed in her response to my audience. She wasn't on my side. She had no mercy for me. She didn't want to come to my pity party.

Linda wasn't playing with me at all. She left the stage, walked down what seemed like a long aisle, and headed right toward me. She was a short woman with lots of power in her walk, her arms swinging with a drill sergeant stiffness, her eyes locked on me and mine on her. She got into my personal space, I stepped back, she stepped forward. I was stuck. My audience had abandoned me.

Linda asked, "What are you really saying here?" I was dead silent. I was feeling confusion, fear and anger. I grabbed my chest. She moved my hand. "Tell me Raquel, what are you really saying?" Linda said in a soft, matter-of-fact tone.

I took time not because I wanted to but because I was searching for an answer. It was a long, very uncomfortable silent pause. The audience was feeling the discomfort too, I could see through my peripheral vision. Some of them were churning in their seats, sweating it out for me. My eyes were still locked on Linda. They were all in the background, silent and probably shocked.

After what felt like an eternity, a river of words flowed out. I connected the dots of using excuses to protect me from living to my maximum potential. I was afraid of failing and afraid of succeeding. I told myself if I failed, it would hurt and others would be disappointed in me. If I succeeded, I had to show all the way up, every day, because the opportunity called for a big fish in a big pond. I was playing on a minnow egg's level and Linda knew it.

TURN ON THAT LIGHT

When I got real with myself in that room in front of 300 others a light went on in my life and it's still shining today. It's more luminous now because I mandated a stop to fear. I made a choice to acknowledge the truth of the matter. I mastered it. The mastery has come through an accountability system of checks and balances that I practice each time superficial self-talk rises. While negative thoughts can be attached to any emotion, if you dig down deep enough, you will more often than not find fear as the common denominator.

In a lot of the books and articles I've read everyone seems to be preaching the same sermon: There's nothing to fear but fear itself or the only real failure is the failure to try and blah, blah, blah. These words are nice and sweet but I'm not buying it. They are comforting but they don't move us to take responsibility for our own stuff. You have to own fear or it will own you.

It is normal to experience fearful feelings. It's normal to want to retreat to a snug space. Scientists and medical doctors agree that our brains have an automatic defense mechanism. When it feels fear, it goes into protective mode and seeks safety. If you are working on stretch assignments out of your comfort zone, fear naturally rises. The brain senses it and sends a note: Return to safety.

Try building a new "Return to safety" response and watch your life expand in ways you couldn't have fathomed. Because fear rushes in as a defense, you won't remove it entirely from your life, but there are some steps you can take to tackle it.

ENOUGHNESS TOOL #4:
KNOW YOURSELF REALLY WELL

Step 1: Gain Clarity. "What are you really saying here?" was Linda's way of saying "What are you afraid of?" Clarity is the first step in establishing a face-off with fear. You might linger in confusion or you might even do it in front of 300 people. Stay with it until you figure it out. What. Are. You. Really. Saying. Here. Best-selling author Deepak Chopra says we have to get clear about our fears if we want to reign over them: "If you try to get rid of fear and anger without knowing their meaning, they will grow stronger and return."

Step 2: Personal Courage. Have the guts to call it what it is. Example: Unbeknownst to me, I was struggling with accepting my personal power. I was suppressing abilities that hadn't yet surfaced. I used excuses to cover up true feelings. Fearful living isn't pretty. You can look good on the outside but if you lack the ability to do right by yourself on the inside you are only fooling yourself. Have a face-off with fear. Use courage.

Step 3: Be Accountable. I did this to myself. I created the internal dialogue of pity and anger and blaming others. I did it. Whether it was consciously or unconsciously, I took it on. Develop an honor code for yourself. Burn the boat. Successful people cut off all communication between head trash and naysayers. They don't look to the left or right. Cut off all ties with the thoughts you allow to dictate your life. You are the master of your thoughts, so master them.

Step 4: Learn Your History: Fear is linked to a history. History is in the past, it has nothing to do with the present moment unless you allow it. From this day forward if you decide to pull fear out of last week into this week, that's on you. You are making a choice to make it real and block the goodness that you so very much deserve.

Step 5: Be Realistic: When fear controls you, ask yourself what emotion you want to feel instead. Want to feel confident instead? Stand up. Walk like a confident person. Get in the groove, head up, shoulders back, belly in. Breathe like a confident person. Speak, sit and eat like one. If you don't feel like doing this exercise, know this: You can absolutely change your emotional state by changing your body language. There is a connection between your mind and body and you are holding the remote control to initiate fast change. Change your state of mind, change the outcome.

Life is Short. You Will Mess Up. Suck it Up.

TAKING RISKS

If you aren't taking risks, you are stagnant. You are stuck. Life is small, and you are surrounded by other small players. It's called the littlest little league. You're dragging your bag through a playground when you should be on that field making plays, scoring points and leading the team huddle. You can tell yourself to be positive and stay inspired but if you aren't taking action, it's all fluff.

When I'm clear of the fluff and on the brink of taking on a big risk, my heart pounds and rolls into somersaults. At times it feels as though I'm sitting on a cold steel rail on a bridge 300 feet above dark water, my feet dangling beneath an unsteady hind end. It is both horribly frightening and exhilarating. I'm scared of screwing up and making a fool of myself and also I'm excited about not screwing up, I'm excited about the possibility of succeeding. But it's the idea of being fulfilled by success that wins me over. Being entrenched in the possibility of success is what pulls me through.

When I started my women's conference, I took more risks that year than I had during the several years prior. I received more "no's" than ever before but that comes with putting yourself out there. It is part of the process. There is no way around it. Risk and rejection pair nicely. They are wonderful travel companions as we chart a new direction. Use them for what they are: Actionable Aids.

I learned to dive off that damn bridge by reconnecting to a little girl who was as brave as anyone I have met: Me. The younger version of me didn't see it as risk-taking. I was too young to understand fear or danger, even when adults forewarned me.

NAIVE, COURAGEOUS OR BOTH

When I was a kid my mother bought me a purple bike. When it glistened in the sun, I thought it had special powers until I got older and realized it was wrapped in a shimmering paint. But in my young mind, it was the most beautiful bike in the neighborhood. My mother smiled as she turned the handlebars my way and said, "Have fun and remember, no riding in the street and stay off Harker Hill."

Off to Harker Hill I went. It was nothing more than a paved street with one traffic light and a steep hill that made any kid drool at the thought of conquering it on a bike, especially a new bike. To make sure I was following some sense of my mother's advice, I safely moved my new ride onto the sidewalk. My heart was pounding. This was my moment. It was my turn to try the hill that every kid in the neighborhood had boasted about. You hadn't really done anything good in life unless you had taken your bike down Harker Hill.

I went for it. Ponytails flying in the air behind me, randomly tapping my back. Purple and white streamers attached to the handlebars fluttering madly. I felt free. The early evening sun warmed my face. It was summer, I was a kid on a new bike and everything was right in the world. Until I hit the bottom of the hill.

At the bottom was a small patch of tiny rocks and dirt. I was an inexperienced cyclist and I certainly hadn't mastered how to brake after the momentum from a monster like Harker Hill. That hill, by the way, is almost non-existent through my adult lens. I hit the pavement sideways, skidding across the concrete. When I came to a stop the world fell eerily quiet. I was alone.

I started to cry but a voice flashed to the front of my head like a wave crashing on a big rock: "Don't you dare cry for falling, you're OK!" I sucked up the tears and opted for bravery.

With a bruised shoulder, knee and ego, I stood up. I began the long limp home rolling my sparkling bike beside me. I wondered if I were in trouble with my mother and I wondered when I could get back on my bike and try it again. Or maybe I should never try it again. I thought about other kids, how they maneuvered through patches of rocks and sand just fine. I was hopeful someone would help me figure it all out before I grew up. The moment I wheeled into my front yard and saw my mother's face, there it was: The longest cry in the world, one long, whiny cry that lasted at least 20 minutes.

After getting some tender loving care from my mother, I realized that I did it! I did what I had been dreaming of and was afraid to do. While it wasn't a total success, I did it. I realized the area I needed to work on: braking after high speed and how to ride through a patch of gravel.

BUILDING THAT COURAGE MUSCLE

I think of this and similar stories when the thought of running from a challenge enters my mind. It's just a thought, it only attaches to meaning if I allow it. Recalling days of bravery allows me to recall experiences where fear didn't yet exist, when it was a foreign concept. When fear isn't present, it leaves room for other things to manifest.

Those little moments of firsts help build courage. We all have them. We have many of them. Every single one of those moments builds character and skill. We often don't realize the importance of them, but they are precious.

But the rose-colored glasses do come off. Fear finds us and we try our best to handle it during our adolescent years on throughout our 20s and beyond. It's rough when the real world isn't as loving as a caring parent who thinks you are super fantastically great. We get emotional bruises from this stuff, we cry at home, in cold, metal bathroom stalls or over a drink in an old, dimly lit, greasy smelling bar.

As we work our way past eight years old and then 10 and 12, we stop learning from our missteps and start seeing our mistakes as bad, unproductive things. We start finding what's wrong and we make that mean something. We stop taking risks and start following others. We lose (and abuse) ourselves in the process.

REFUELING THROUGH RISK

Risk taking is one of the fastest ways to refuel self-worth. It is the juice in the berry, the yolk in the egg. It shakes us. Taking risks is a brave action. Be brave. It's not easy and doesn't have to be pretty. Be ready to mess some things up. It is filled with uncertainty which can lead to a significant amount of fear. It's OK to feel this way. Be with it. The head trash we've collected keeps us numb to the idea that fear can be a good thing. At first, you might believe that your comfort zone is a better place to reside. Don't bet on it. Comfort zones are traps for risk takers. You can't nestle there. You have to cancel your membership in that club if you desire significant progress.

With risk taking, we don't know anything for sure and again, that's OK. We are blindly dancing through a forest with frightening terrain and hidden gems. This is exactly where you want to be if you plan to win. Don't let self-defeating thoughts steer you away from this truth.

Be careful with fear. It can sometimes transform into other emotions to make us feel better temporarily. For example, some people are striving for the pursuit of excellence and in that pursuit they give themselves a pass to prolong or fall off the journey. They tell themselves, "If I'm right for the job or promotion, they will find me."

No, "they" probably won't find you.

In all your greatness, and you are great, you cannot depend on others to take notice. You cannot rely on their awareness of you to create your opportunities. This is a false belief that you will be noticed and the influencers will find you. Yes, it can happen, but why depend solely on it? Chances are you could spend years waiting for someone to spot your brilliance. You can wait it out until a new owner or management team comes in but you're right back where you started; proving yourself all over again.

Why place your future in the hands of someone else who is just awakening to your Enoughness? Take the wheel. Take it now.

RUNNING OUT OF TIME

When you feel fear rushing in, consider the master that you have no control over: Time. Which scares you the most: fear or running out of time?

Your answer should be: time. Here's why. One day there will be a final one. You will take a final walk, you will have a final meal, you will buy a final pair of shoes, you will say a final "I love you," and you will take a final breath. It's going to happen to each of us. Each day we get closer to that final day. Each day we grow closer to the day when our heart and voice will be silenced.

We don't know when this big silencing is going to happen. You know the expiration date of your credit cards, library books and milk but you don't know your personal expiration date. Since you don't know it, each day should count, each day should be meaningful. We should strive to live deeply and completely each day.

So today is really all we have. Yesterday is a wrap and tomorrow isn't even a thing; it's only a hope. We can only count on today. There is no other time to start taking bigger risks and tackling projects on your list. Start where you are right now.

ENOUGHNESS TOOL #5: ASSESS YOUR 'COST OF LIVING'
Step 1: Grab paper and a pen, and draw a vertical line down the middle of the page. At the top of the page write the goal. On the left side of the page write: Costs of Doing it. On the right side write: Payoffs of Doing it. Write down every conceivable thought you have about what this goal will cost you if you do it. Do the same with the payoffs. Example, it may cost you displeasure in giving up buying a coffee to save money or it may cost you discomfort to play big. Write it all down.

Step 2: Flip the page over, same thing: line down the middle, write the same goal at the top of the page. On the left side of the page write: Costs of NOT Doing it. Right side: Payoffs of NOT Doing it. Same as above, write it down, be frantic and fast. What is the cost of not doing it? Is living with regret one of the costs or being ticked off after someone else steals your idea? What is a payoff of not doing it, do you stay small in the littlest little league?

Step 3: Do this with each project. It not only sharpens your focus on why you need to take action, it sets up a realistic view of what it will look like if you don't do it. There are no surprises when you feel angered by sitting on a sideline because you already know what's going to happen if you don't take action. This exercise calls us out to either play big or go home. There is no gray area.

Take this exercise and decide which column you're going to live in today and with the time you have left on earth. Make a definitive decision that this is how you choose to approach risks and deal with whatever drama unfolds. And don't think this is doable only for younger folks. It works for you now.

THIS COULD BE **YOU**!

It works for women in their 30s, 40s, 50s, 60s and beyond. There is a long list of women who have succeed at different times in life. Here are a few of my favorites.

Viola Davis: Unlike many actresses in Tinseltown, Davis wasn't a breakout child star or a young bombshell. While highly educated, she made her Broadway debut at the age of 31. But it wasn't until she received an Academy Award nomination for Best Supporting Actress for the film Doubt that people knew her name. She was 43. Her career took off and so did her fame.

Lucille Ball: She was once asked to leave drama school for her failure to perform. Thank goodness she didn't listen. Through a career of highs and lows, Ball landed on high ground with the first season of I Love Lucy. She was 40.

Martha Stewart: She had some success working on Wall Street and in a catering firm. She seemed to always have a career of some sort. Stewart's life changed when she published her first book and America fell in love with her. She was 41.

Julia Child: She was not born a cook. Child didn't learn to cook until she was 36 after taking a six-month French cooking course. She became a cooking sensation after her first book hit the shelves followed by a TV show. She wrote the book at 40.

Joy Behar: Best known for her role as co-host on The View, she was a high school English teacher before launching a show business career. Behar traded in her textbooks after the age of 40 and she's still telling her view point well into her 70s.

Vera Wang: Before becoming an international designer, Wang was gliding on ice as a figure skater. She didn't have any thoughts about bridal wear until she was planning her own wedding at the age of 40. Frustrated with the lack of design options, Wang spun into action and began designing her own gowns and as they say, the rest is HERstory.

Lynda Weinman: A self-taught computer whiz and former graphic arts professor solved a need in 1995 by writing a book on graphic design. She sold hundreds of thousands of copies and shortly thereafter started Lynda.com, an Internet based training company. She was 40. The company was sold to LinkedIn in April 2015 for $1.5 billion.

Judy Sheindlin: Best known by her on-screen moniker, Judge Judy, the sharp-tongued ruler wasn't always a hit. Sheindlin worked in law for decades but her big break came in 1996 with a court program. Now, over 20 seasons later and millions of dollars richer, Sheindlin has a success story. She was 52 when the show started.

Jill Boehler: For three decades she worked in speech pathology. It was during her early 50s that Boehler got a rather chilling idea. After sitting in a cold restaurant she was inspired to create a product that would lead her to become an entrepreneur. She developed a wrap, Chilly Jilly, in 2007 and sold thousands of the garments in boutiques, online, and through QVC.

Carol Gardner: Reportedly Gardner hit rock bottom at the age of 52. She divorced her husband, bought a dog, and entered a contest sponsored by the local pet store. She won and became inspired to create Zelda Wisdom, a unique greeting card company. She gained the attention of Hallmark and now sells gifts, clothing, jewelry, calendars, and books.

ENTER YOUR NAME AND BLURB HERE,
WRITE YOUR SUCCESS STORY:

Be Memorable. Foster conversations that strengthen yourself and others. Charge yourself with the task of creating an atmosphere that uplifts humanity and focuses on common good.

NetWORKing

Think about it; you are connecting with a stranger, the same thing your parents warned you about when you were a child. While our parents wanted to protect us from kidnappers (and boys), we built up fear about people we didn't know.

Now, we are bigger, stronger human beings with families, cars and lots and lots of shoes. We are responsible adults with many successes tucked in our achievement bag. We lift weights, travel, feed dolphins, hike up mountains, and volunteer in third world countries but we are nervous about meeting strangers at a happy hour networking function.

The first thing we do is ask friends to meet us there. No way are we going it alone. We need a buffer, preferably a long-winded one, in case it doesn't work out. We might cancel if our buffer buddy can't make it. That is simply nonsense. How we think and feel about network is holding our ideas, innovations and desire to advance hostage. You've got to network.

Beyond the handshakes, collecting business cards and beverage tickets is a unique opportunity to engage with a perfect stranger. We're being vulnerable in a sense because we're sharing parts of ourselves without knowing the outcome. It is intimate and for some, damn scary.

The moment you walk into the room you notice the cliques of people tied at the hip. Have you ever tried to elbow your way into their conversation? Yikes! They all stop talking and snap their heads in your direction, staring as if you have slime dripping from your face. You are not the horror film star here. It is the people who attend networking events and only network with people they already know who are the real stars of the horror film.

Networking isn't a party. It's work. It is results driven work.

The objective is to ignite conversations that foster future relationships. It is working toward a shared goal. It has the potential to be a win-win situation for everyone involved.

I see a network as a circle. Each person you add to your circle helps complete it. The network builds a circle around you. They are there to support your ideas and help open doors along the way. When you become part of someone else's network, a new link in their circle, you return the favor.

NETWORKING IS A LEARNED SKILL

When I decided to take the leap and start my company after my tenure in TV news, I had to learn how to network. When I lived in Dallas and other markets, networking wasn't a priority because the communities I served were familiar with me from seeing me on the evening newscast.

When I left all of that behind and returned to Ohio, no one knew my face or social status. I couldn't get the meetings to gain support for my women's conference project. I couldn't get past the gatekeeper or even her gatekeeper. I had to start from scratch.

Armed with a stack of business cards tied in a rubber band and an equally tight knot in my stomach, I started the long walk (a whole forty seconds max) from the parking lot to the front door of restaurants, chamber meetings and awards banquets. Inside, the rooms had lots of nervous laughter and clammy handshakes. Most people looked as uncomfortable as I felt.

About two months into this networking game, I was coming up with blanks. I was attracting the wrong people. While I tried to talk myself into making a connection with each person I met, the truth was, a lot of them were wrong for me and I for them. That means I wasted time. I was on the fast track to achieving my goals. I had a plan. What I didn't have was time to waste.

While I was attending a women's luncheon in a small, quiet part of town a woman approached me about selling her makeup line for her. I quietly said, "No thank you." A few minutes later, while I was en route to the bathroom another woman stopped me and said in a high-pitched, super excited tone, "Let's have coffee!!!" She forced her card into my hand. I inquired about the reason for our meeting. She said, "Let's have coffee about coffee! I have a network marketing coffee business you'd be perfect for, are you looking for an opportunity?" I said I was looking for an opportunity but this "ain't it." I bypassed the bathroom and headed for the bright exit sign, then got into my car with a full bladder and sped through a retirement community. I was done.

Just like that, a total of four hours was gone. After adding in travel time to and from the event itself, it was too much time to invest for minimum rewards. I changed my approach to not only how I network but with whom I network.

THE POWER OF A PLAN

My new strategy afforded me the opportunity to get in the right room with the right people. By right, I mean people who had similar interests as me, those who had passion for equality, diversity and inclusion and women's empowerment. Once in the right room, I had to introduce myself into groups of chatty folks. I had to initiative conversations and listen intently for similar points of reference. Being in influential rooms also means that you may be the one who has to follow up. If that is the case, then do it. Do what you have to do to broaden opportunities and attach yourself to worthy causes and people who will take a chance on you.

Still, all of that work was a process and it was a slow moving one at that. I'm not the girl who sits on her hands watching grass grow. I have to be moving forward. So while people were warming up to me, I was on fire.

When I wasn't getting invited to meetings, I hosted my own meeting. When you want a network and the doors aren't opening as you desire, make the first move, open the damn door.

I started with small mastermind groups in my home. I scheduled dinners at restaurants with two or three people at a time. I had a plan for the conversation. People were engaged and happy to contribute to the topic. I didn't allow other things to get in the way of scheduling these meetings or hosting them. At the time, the condition of my home was lackluster as I was still recovering from financial hardships. That didn't matter, I had work to do. I didn't have lots of cash, so I'd charge the dinners and strategically schedule them during happy hour for great pricing (there was never a steak or lobster on that menu).

Networking was my way of building my business. It was also my way of becoming more involved in the community I wanted to serve. Establishing meaningful relationships both professional and personal brings incredible value to your life. Every source of value contributes to your Enoughness.

Connecting with others can be exciting. Each event can be a unique experience. You can enhance your ability to connect with others in a way that positively impacts them and yourself. Use networking to boost your confidence level and bottom line. You can move from networking to exploring new ideas and helping your organization evolve. You can also seek ways to help contribute to the success of others.

The following checklist is a guide for you to network with ease. It's a way for you to be memorable long after the event is over.

ENOUGHNESS TOOL #6: NETWORK WITH PURPOSE
1. Bypass the Virtual Process: Clicking on your social media network isn't networking. Research shows that we ignite deeper connections with people during personal interactions. Our brains releases oxytocin, a powerful hormone that regulates social interactions, when we connect face to face. Get out there!

2. Monitor Self Esteem: You have it in you, the belief in your ability to succeed. You know you can do it. Envision yourself at events creating empowering conversations and adding value to others. Your sense of self esteem can play a major role in how you approach networking.

3. Seek Success Through Silence: Connecting requires dialogue but intentional listening is what nurtures opportunities. Find a way to listen more than you speak. Let others know you're interested in them. You'll learn more by listening instead of hearing yourself talk aimlessly about work and family.

4. Be Intentional When Connecting: Get clear on what you want your network to do for you and how you want to help others. Once you identify your goals, execute through a lively exchange of thoughts and ideas with your new contact. Make your time together mean something other than a casual meeting at an event.

5. Be Inclusive: Networking fosters a strong sense of community. Break out of the norm of speaking only with people who look like you. Challenge yourself to network with other cultures and ethnicities. When we learn more about each other's differences, we empower ourselves to be a voice of cultural diversity which will expand our influence.

6. Stay Engaged: Don't wait for an invitation, it likely won't come. It's not unethical to initiate strong follow-ups. Turn your follow-ups into follow-throughs. The day following the event, send an email or even better, a physical note or card of gratitude. Build your way up to chatting over coffee or sharing some time together at the next event. Be diligent by sending gentle notes of interest.

You Had it All Along

PART TWO: BE WISE

Authentic wisdom can't be bought. You can only earn it. There are both gentle and harsh teachers all around you waiting to unveil the next reward. Our job is not to rush wisdom in. We have a much bigger job: Wait, listen and be ready. That's it.

We think that wisdom is about soundness of mind or making good judgment. In many cases it is just the opposite. We become wise through an array of experiences. From life's big moments to those inconsequential ones, they all have a job to do. Let them do their job. The greatness that flows into your life is also a pathway to wisdom. Love, compassion and humility increase your poise. Every incident of bad blood, hostility and boiling anger also leads to mental acuity. Challenges tend to take us into a more profound act of self-reflection because we experience emotions that sting. As pain grasps our attention, we are alert students when hurt or humiliation kicks in. Embrace the learning curve, it will serve you well. Commit to it.

The problem is not in letting wisdom in. The problem for most of us is the time and experiences tied to it. It is all the strife we endure to earn our stripes. The fear of how much it might hurt and how much we will lose in the process is what really frightens us. Gaining insight is not complicated and it doesn't take a lot of time.

Use your vision to expedite wisdom. What do you want for yourself? What is your destination? When will you arrive? Why haven't you arrived yet? What is your current navigational system? And the most important question: why? why does it matter? what is your reason behind it all?

USE YOUR WHY

Instead of being focused on the "what," author and motivational speaker Simon Sinek narrows his focus solely on the "why." In a 2010 How Great Leaders Inspire Action TED Talk, he told over 37 million viewers how inspired leaders communicate from within. Sinek took a simple thought and brilliantly explained how our brains interpret the why, the how and the what, and how we respond to each. "People don't buy what you do but why you do it." So there is no point is spending more energy figuring out the how and the what. Don't affix any limits to those. Instead laser focus your internal guidance system. Dial it in. Be true to your beliefs, and inspire others along the way.

You are a savvy traveler and the items in your Enoughness bag are the perfect complement. Your wisdom compartment is no exception. It is lined with the finest materials to protect your pearls of wisdom. The fabric is breathable to allow the natural rhythm of life to flow. This section of your bag is expandable to support the many merits you currently have and the ones you have yet to discover.

Each section in Be Wise is intended to delicately and swiftly move you closer to your inner wisdom. It's there, even if you haven't been acquainted as of late. Believe that it is there. Believe that you are impeccable. Believe that you deserve it. The sooner you reconnect with that brilliant built-in compass the sooner you can get on with your travel plans to your chosen destination and the sooner you can handle the expected and surprise turbulences.

Lead with compassion and love.
Validating others builds trust and likeability.

EMOTIONAL INTELLIGENCE

Emotional intelligence (EI) is necessary for success. If this skill is not strong, you will struggle to communicate well with others, and people will not feel at ease with you. The EI journey is a hard one. It is challenging because of the high-pressure nature of American culture. People are rushed and frazzled. They are unfocused and naturally low on EI. Another reason why we are not using our emotional intelligence meter is because it requires a high degree of self-awareness requiring plenty of patience. Patience with yourself and others.

If you aren't in control of your emotions, I can guarantee that someone else has control over them. Someone else is sounding the bells and whistles, yanking your chain and testing your nerves. Why leave such an important task to chance?

When I realized I was giving others permission to tell me how to feel and how to respond I was shocked. But it was something I could fix. Sometimes it just takes time to realize what you are allowing. We get it when we get it. And when we get it, we make the necessary changes needed to get us to where we want to be.

We have to control our own emotions.

A rock climber can't control the mountain, but he can accurately order his step. He chooses his thoughts during the climb. A whitewater rafter can't control the water but she can manage her emotions to navigate the course successfully. You too have the capability to make decisions about your reactions to things that you have no control over.

That's what EI is, the ability to be aware of and control your emotions. Empathy, compassion and grace are at the base of it. EI is an in-depth look at how you interpret and manage your way through your career, relationships and your life.

USING EI TO BREAK DOWN BARRIERS

I realized that my emotional intelligence lever had kicked into high gear when I was working with a group of executives during a three-day leadership training. The group was a mixture of men and women who worked for an organization helping disenfranchised residents. Their workload was heavy.

One woman, a decorated army veteran, was as tough as nails. Nothing got to her. She was strong at the start of my program and had buried herself behind an even stronger wall of cement as we neared the completion. Many of her colleagues were having a difficult time working with her. She questioned me on every principle I taught. At times she became a distraction.

When I began to talk about owning up to mistakes with your team, that hit her button. She asked for a one-on-one conversation with me during the break. I was relieved to see a small opening in that wall.

Instead of being frustrated with her demeanor, I approached her concerns with compassion. I listened with empathy. I asked questions about the issues that were important to her. I stepped down from my agenda of leading an insightful forum and focused solely on this woman. I knew my work in developing EI had indeed paid off.

In the end I discovered the woman was raised by tough, military parents who taught structure and perfection. In her world it was not OK to make mistakes and there surely wasn't room to own up to errors. The only way to learn this part of her history was by being self aware, without judgment.

PROCESSING MACHINES

We spend a lot of time processing thoughts and the meanings we give those thoughts. We make judgments on ourselves based on how we feel. We judge others based on how we interpret their reaction, and we accuse them of making us feel a particular way.

There is so much to filter through in the Emotional Intelligence realm. You have to decipher what the truth is and be accountable for your feelings and interpretations. You also need to be mindful of all the history that comes into play when you deal with others: cultural differences, backstories, points of view, etc.

PEOPLE CONNECTOR MUSCLE

Emotional Intelligence is my "people connector muscle." It helps me relate to others quickly and effectively. For me, the majority of people have always connected with my emotional plea over my theoretical one.

During a keynote presentation at an academic leadership summit one fall, I designed my 20-minute speech from an EI perspective. I appealed to the emotional side of the audience. The ballroom was filled with women in academia, industry and college students all from different age groups.

I used personal stories to connect with the audience and asked more questions such as have any of you been in this position before and do you know how it feels when…? Women nodded their heads while others spoke our directly, "Yes, I have!" A few women gave each other a fist bump. When I spoke the room was silent; when I asked for confirmation, they yelled it out.

The afternoon keynote, a highly degreed woman from the east coast, delivered a more theoretical approach. Her approach was different. It was more of a lecture. I have to admit, I was a bit lost while listening to her and I wondered if the participants felt the same.

After the event many attendees spoke with me and I noticed an instant connection. Most of them were repeating terms and themes I had used through my speech, which is a telltale sign that people are not only hearing you but they are traveling down your journey with you. And without my prompting, they expressed feeling less of a connection with the other speaker. The written surveys were equally favorable for my presentation.

This isn't a toot of the horn, but an important lesson on how to engage with people from different backgrounds and perhaps different interests than you. The scholarly speaker may have received higher marks if the audience consisted of people in her field or scholar level. If you want to relate to anyone and nearly everyone, EI is the way to do it.

START WITH SELF-AWARENESS

The pathway to an Emotional Intelligence state is through self-awareness. It is the first step. Self-awareness begins with mindfulness. Be mindful of how you interpret experiences, responses and your reactions. It's your job to be on point with this. You are the only one who can manage it. Everything in my life has an action and reaction; I may not be able to control the action of what happened but I am 100% responsible for controlling my reaction. I'll talk more about mindfulness in the next section but for now get comfortable with the idea of being very present as you strive to elevate your EI.

The Harvard Business Review, like so many other scholarly institutions, has its own EI model. I like the HBR's model because it dives deeper than the empathetic level. This compass points you in the direction of being able to navigate through the real world without becoming a doormat. Their formula widens the focus on EI and uses a four-pillar approach: self-awareness, self-management, social awareness, and relationship management. Inside each pillar are a dozen competencies which I urge you to review in the Resources section of this book.

It's not only about emotional aptitude but skills. I like to think of it as using your heart and brain simultaneously to get the desired result and treat everyone well in the process, including yourself.

ENOUGHNESS TOOL #7:
STRENGTHEN SELF-AWARENESS

In the Resources section of this book you'll find a guide to the four pillars: Self-Awareness, Self-Management, Social Awareness, and Relationship Management. Research them. For now, let's work on what I call the founding father of EI: Self-Awareness.

1. Ask Yourself: What's in my control? Naturally, your responses and reactions are in your control.

2. Do a Self Check: With the above information, gauge how you interpreted a recent situation. Were you aware of all the filters in your backstory, the points of view that make up your reality? Were you aware of how your point of view vastly differed from other people involved? (This doesn't make it wrong or right, just different.)

3. Prepare for Future Engagement: How can you bring a positive response to each situation? Go through the above steps before your meeting. Do this each time you want to tap into your EI. Train your brain to make the end result a positive one. Always end on a high note.

You've already built the stage, now perform on it.

CONFIDENCE

No one cares more about your success than you do. Having confidence is a critical part of developing personal and professional fortitude.

Confidence is the byproduct of living a good life. You find great fulfillment in creating happiness and accomplishing goals. Most of the highly successful people you read about in articles or see in interviews are self-assured based on the life they have created for themselves. All of this takes confidence, or as I like to call it, guts.

What's interesting about confidence is you either have it or you do not. Either way, it takes effort. It takes some work getting there and the opposite is also true; you have to work at being less confident too.

You can move yourself away from your boldness by criticizing yourself or your self-image. It takes time and great effort to be negative towards life circumstances or to doubt goodness. Talking yourself out of being a candidate for the promotion is not an easy task; it takes work.

When you are unsure of yourself, nothing seems to work out to your benefit. It seems that everyone else is winning. You start the day stale instead of excited. Ending the day feels like a chore instead of a blessing. There are many negative feelings involved. Living like this hinders healthy emotions. We miss out on the excitability and joy of life. We might put on a good face for others, but we feel like an elephant is sitting on our chest. It's hard to move, breathe or simply live.

Beulah put on a good face, it was the same face day after day, year after year. She wanted others to buy into her happy-go-lucky attitude but inside she was unraveling and I witnessed it firsthand.

I lived in the same house my entire childhood, surrounded by the same neighbors. No one moved away and no one moved in. We were a close-knit community. Our front doors were always unlocked. You were welcomed and so was Beulah.

Beulah was a stout woman with dark, smooth skin and large, protruding eyes. She wore wide skirts with sandals and at times silk scarves tied around her head. She had a big mouth and it was a good thing because she also had a big voice. Beulah was a singer and her raspy voice could compete with the best of them.

We had an old piano in one corner of our dining room. And though no one in the house knew how to play more than one tune, Beulah, who lived across town, knew that piano inside and out.

PLAYING FOR AN AUDIENCE OF ONE
You were never prepared for Beulah's visit because she always arrived unannounced. The only signal we had was the sound of her singing from down the street. Her voice would get closer and closer, on the porch, in the front door, through the living room and to that piano, occasionally humming a few hello's along the way. She was doing what we called 'sang'in.' It was deep and soulful. She composed some original songs as well as harmonizing some R&B renditions of Diana Ross, Aretha Franklin and others. She would shake her head swaying the thick, long locks attached to her wig. You could tell she meant every word in those lyrics. She owned them. Sometimes my family would gather around her and other times she would play alone. I was always nearby. Standing with my hands covering my mouth, in awe of the beauty of this strange woman's vocals.

When she played without the audience, she often cried. She was emotional and I was told to let Ms. Beulah be. "She has problems," my great-grandmother said.

I was no more than eight or nine years old when Beulah started this little showcase in my dining room. It continued on through my high school years. As I got older I spoke to people who knew Beulah well.

I wanted to know more about her talent and tears.

According to people who knew and loved her, Beulah was offered a few chances to go to Detroit and record at Motown. Everything was paid for, all she had to do was show up and sing. She had an opportunity to work with Smokey Robinson who was writing one hit record after another. But Beulah never took that 2+ hour drive up north. She would only walk across town to sing out her blues in our dimly-lit dining room on our old piano.

OPPORTUNITY WAITS FOR NO ONE

Finally, after Motown invited her to their studio, they stopped calling and stopped taking her calls. They pulled the offer. Beulah spiraled out of control. She would later tell me that everyone believed in her, everyone except Beulah. She lacked confidence in herself. No matter how beautiful her deep, rhythmic voice was, she didn't see it that way. No one could convince her otherwise. She wasn't open to receiving those types of messages.

You have to do more than know what you do well, you have to believe it. You cannot leave it to others to validate your talent or ability. Your cheerleaders will take you only so far. You've got to be the one out there on the court, taking the shots, scoring the points, and getting a little roughed up.

Confident people aren't afraid of hardships. To get to success, they run through the rejection wringer. But they don't take it personally and they don't bow out of the game. They might take a step back, reframe the situation and make another attempt but they don't stop. You can't start singing around the corner and open the front door and play to an audience of one. You have to use that as practice and then take the longer ride for the success you yearn for.

A lot of work goes into making you. Think of your value system, your beliefs, the personal and professional development training you've invested in. All of it has started somewhere and has gotten you to where you are today.

CONFIDENCE OPENS DOORS

Being bold and self-reliant is a strong base for an exhilarating life. You are unstoppable! Even with rejection, you keep it moving. Once you get into a groove you'll be pleasantly surprised to know that the more confidence you build the less rejection you experience. Confidence is like a magnet; people are drawn to the energy.

Successful businesses and careers thrive because of confident leaders. The same is true for good marriages and parenthood. When you remove doubt and bring a positive vibration into life the vibe is infectious. Other people want to be around it. They like you and you like you too.

If you really want to get this confident thing flowing, you need to contribute to your personal account. You must make a deposit every single day. Think of confidence as a muscle. Flex it every day, every chance you get.

BELIEVE IT OR NO ONE ELSE WILL

R&B recording artist Patti LaBelle's powerful voice and confident demeanor have always intrigued me. I've never seen her fall short of excellent.

During a sit-down interview with the award-winning artist, I asked Ms. Patti if she knew she was going to be this famous and fabulous. She paused for a moment, started to speak, then hesitated. It sounded to me as if she was going to respond the way people might expect her to with a kind and gracious response. Truthfully, that would have surprised me because a woman with such talent and accolades must have the belief to back it all up. Right?

Ms. Patti simply said, "Let me stop player hating (throwing negativity on yourself or others), yes I knew it, I knew I was going to make it. It was very hard work but I knew I was good and was going to make it." We laughed and gave each other a high five. I was so glad to hear her give it up for herself.

There are many ways you can build more confidence. These suggestions might sound like work and they are. This isn't one of those home improvement shows where everything is done by the end of the 30-minute show. A lot of work goes on behind the scenes that viewers don't see.

ENOUGHNESS TOOL #8:
FIVE WAYS TO BUILD CONFIDENCE

1. Be Decisive: Don't give it a second thought. Play yourself up with every opportunity. When someone compliments your attire, say "Thank you" instead of, "Oh this old thing…" Confident people really like themselves. They freely give and accept positive remarks.

2. Commit to Pushing Yourself: Join Toastmasters or anything that pushes you to interact with other professionals through unrehearsed public speaking. Do a quick search for the nearest Toastmaster club in your area. Jump in on one of their table topics exercises. Each go at it will increase confidence. I promise.

3. Create Your Vision: Understanding your purpose will unlock productivity and inspire results. If you can't see it, it's hard to believe it. Feed your confidence with a daily dose of visual stimulation.

4. Create a Vision Board: Post daily reminders of your purpose on a vision board. Clip photos and quotes from articles or magazines that align with your goals and beliefs. Don't just look at it daily, study it, drool over it. Let your work area fill up your Enoughness with things that spark you.

5. Have Fun! Packing more confidence in your bag is a good thing so enjoy it. It's a gift that keeps on giving.

Playing small doesn't serve the world

VOICE LESSONS

You want to say it but you don't. You should have said it but you didn't. You wanted to back up a colleague but you couldn't. You didn't defend yourself. You kept quiet, afraid that you might be wrong or you might end up alone.

The words aren't escaping you, your voice is.

I've heard from many women who work in male-dominated industries about the unsettling task of speaking up. They weren't having difficulty finding the words, the problem was collecting the courage to say them. Feelings of uncertainty or fear keep us quiet.

I've been there: the thought on the tip of my tongue but I retreated. I could feel my inner voice burning inside. It felt like I was suffocating my voice. There were times when I lost my voice and couldn't speak. I literally got sick and could not speak. I thought it was a symptom of a virus but it was a different type of sickness. I was in emotional discord with myself. I had closed the door on my Enoughness one too many times. I was in shutdown mode.

SQUANDERING YOUR BIRTHRIGHT

Like so many other women, I was squandering my birthright to be everything I could be. I was storing all my good stuff in an old unclaimed bag in the airport lost and found promising to pick it up when "it felt right" or when "I researched more." In the meantime, newcomers were blossoming all around me. They were pitching the same ideas at meetings that I was secretly recording in a journal I kept at home in my closet. Obviously, that was also where I was keeping my voice because I certainly wasn't using it. My Enoughness bag didn't have many miles on it at all. I knew better, I knew what I had to say would matter but in that particular moment, I could not speak up.

My maternal great-grandmother, who everyone called Mama Eatmon, never once bit her tongue in the 29 years that I knew her. Not once did she neglect her voice. I was amazed by her skill, especially seeing that she grew up in truly challenging times.

USE YOUR BACKSTORY

Mama Eatmon was the granddaughter of slaves. She and her parents picked cotton in the hot fields of Alabama. She married James and made her way to Ohio to start a family. By the time I was born into this family, Mama Eatmon was a true force. It was apparent that her hardships had transformed into strengths. Her voice was unrelenting and everyone in our neighborhood, church and police department knew it. I knew it too and it followed me through my adolescence.

Teen years are awkward enough, and this is even more true when you throw boys into the mix. Anyone who wanted to date me had to visit our home. Friday after school was when they could meet my family. At times, Mama Eatmon was embarrassing. She asked questions and responded directly. She was no sugar coater, not to boys or grown men either.

I would later figure out why male visitors were told to stop by on Fridays. It was a conspiracy. Nearly every Friday my brave and bold great-grandmother would rest herself in front of the T.V. She'd pull that wooden lever on her recliner chair and slide back into a state of relaxation. While it seemed to me she sat there most of the day, I didn't understand the need to downshift gears and sink deeper. But when she slid back, the entire family knew what was happening next. It was not a nap.

She reached her narrow hands down the pouch of the chair and pulled out a small brown paper bag containing a pint of Black Velvet. When she twisted off that top I swear sometimes the un-clicking sound traveled through the entire house as if it was on a high voltage microphone. A good ten minutes later her voice was two octaves higher. She coined this experience as her "Friday Nip." She nipped and we all cringed.

Mama Eatmon was an incredibly strong woman. She survived the deaths of a husband and two children. She a was a churchgoing woman who loved gardening and caring for children. She took in many kids whose parents were dealing with challenging times. She kept them for a week or six months. She was an extremely caring person but she didn't hesitate to speak up. Even through the Friday Nip, she didn't change her position. The pitch of her voice may have been a bit higher but the content of her delivery never wavered.

Those silly boys who came to visit on Friday afternoon didn't have a clue what they were walking into. She asked them point blank about their intentions and at times said, "I don't believe a word you're saying. You don't have me fooled one bit." My uncles and older cousins would gather around for this drill and they would laugh and high five each other when Mama Eatmon spoke her mind.

LET NATURAL BE NATURAL

During one visit with a boy I was quite fond of, Mama Eatmon took a bathroom break. Since the bath was right off the living room you could hear pretty much everything happening between the small walls if it were loud enough. You know where I'm going with this. My tiny grandmother let out a big one, and it was loud. I screamed, "Gross!" She yelled back, "It's not gross, it's natural, let natural be natural!"

She didn't apologize for it being natural. When you think about it, if it's natural, why does it need an apology or explanation or sense of embarrassment?

What was really cool about my great-grandmother's voice was that her Friday Nip didn't shift her tact. She was not a woman who needed liquid courage to handle skinny, hormonal 16-year-old boys or a disgruntled deacon at church. She was the same through it all. She spoke up at Sunday dinner just as much as she did with police officers who stopped her for driving without a license, dozens of times. She knew who she was and she refused to apologize for it. She refused to play a role and be anyone else other than herself.

YOUR VOICE IS WORTH HEARING

Mama Eatmon's voice lessons were ingrained in us girls on a daily basis: Say what needs to be said, when it needs to be said. She was direct, never over-explaining or under-appreciating others. She was perfect.

You have to believe that what you have to say is worth hearing. You have to know that your voice adds color to the conversation. Your point of view is original, it's been marinating and it has flavor. Feed it to the folks.

YOU BELONG IN THE ROOM

You belong in the room. Even if you doubt it, go into the room like you belong. Walk in like a boss. Pretend if you have to but do it anyway. While Mama Eatmon's message was clear, the world has a way of stripping you down from what you know to be true. Once I reconnected with her lessons, I wanted to guide others to do the same.

I added ProjectHeard.com, an online leadership forum, to my business portfolio because I believed the world needed a digital space where women could share their voices. I wanted their stories to be heard in every corner of the world. I wanted to celebrate our voices in leadership, STEM, entrepreneurship, lifestyle and wellness.

And here is another resource for you to pack in your bag.

ENOUGHNESS TOOL #9: FIVE WAYS
TO INTENSIFY YOUR VOICE RIGHT NOW

What are some of your own voice lessons and how are you using your voice to benefit yourself and others? Work this program:

1. Don't Just Stand in Your Truth, Be It: Check in on your values and beliefs. Are you drifting away from your morals and leaning more towards what is popular? Be true to yourself every single day. Be intuitive and follow what feels right for you. Following your intuition gives you one less thing to focus on before you speak up. Part of being heard is speaking from an authentic perspective. Being genuine is also easy to understand. People can tell when you're a fake.

2. Don't Let a Deeper Tone or More Accredited Person Cause You to Second Guess Yourself: I know a lot of super smart people. I surround myself with them because I enjoy learning new things. I have respect for their brilliance but I don't take a second place ribbon just because they have more letters after their names. They don't have my experience or point of view. We see things through a different lens. I don't compare our accomplishments because that is a sure way to lose power. You and I are in the business of collecting power. There is no time to simply give it away.

3. Lend Your Voice to Include Others: I don't enjoy speaking to a room full of people who all look alike. This doesn't reflect the real world. If I'm hosting a women's forum, I want men there, I want white and black women there. Hispanics and Asians. All colors, shapes and sizes. If you find yourself at a table of people who look like you, speak up and ask for diversity. Speak up and question how your team inspires change with a room full of people who do not reflect your clientele or community. Use your voice to help people identify their unconscious biases.

4. Don't Shrink to Make Other People Comfortable: Sometimes people will be uncomfortable with your Enoughness. That is their problem, not yours. You have to bring all of you to the table each time, regardless of how other people can or can not cope with it. Be brilliant, gorgeous, talented and fabulous, and don't wither for anyone. Repeat after me: It's over. It's done. It will never happen again. I will never downplay myself to make others feel more comfortable.

5. Be Compassionately Assertive: You can be loving, thoughtful and generous with your voice. Choose language that celebrates your ability to take ownership over pointing the finger at others. For example, when you're offended by something Fred said at the meeting, speak up. Say: "I was uncomfortable with that phrase you used..." instead of, "You made me feel uncomfortable with that phrase you used." Whenever there is opposition, people usually put up a guard. It's a natural defense mechanism. Taking ownership of your feelings will lighten the exchange. Also consider using your feedback as a way to help others better understand your unique point of view. Allow your voice to unify. Use it to help your team better relate to a diverse range of clients.

Shame has no place to be

SHAME

Shame is a personal persecutor. It causes a terrible erosion of the esteem. It's heavy, hard and sinks all the way to the core. We hide secrets in it. We bear the weight or throw it on the backs of others. It's an emotion that keeps us pointing a finger and playing the blame game.

Feeling a sense of shamefulness was one of the greatest thieves of my life. This is true for many of us. It has stolen time and emotions, and prevented relationships from blossoming. We are good at this shame thing. We shame ourselves and we shame others.

THINGS WE DON'T WANT TO ADMIT

The incidents that cause shamefulness are usually things that we don't want to admit. We mask the abuse that happened. We hide that we were mistreated. We don't want to admit that we didn't or couldn't stand up for ourselves. But it did happen, and we are left with tangled emotions that strengthen shame and pity.

These emotions keep us small inside. They keep us locked in a place where we exhibit all sorts of negative behaviors.

I have tangoed with shame more times than I can count. Some of those moments were very private and others were on a public forum.

Eons ago I won a Miss Ohio pageant and part of that job was playing nice with the public and attending community functions. One particular day I was scheduled for a personal appearance at a city council meeting. I was receiving a certificate from the city, congratulating me on the title. I sat quietly for hours as a small group of men and one woman went back and forth on issues. I was the last item on their agenda.

So there I sat, with my satin and rhinestone sash with the fancy Miss Ohio statement splashed across it. I sat patiently, prim and proper like my mom had taught me.

And for the record let me say that I got involved in the pageantry business strictly for the scholarship dollars. I didn't expect to win as the other girls were prettier than me, and slimmer, and while my golden skin was darker, theirs was a peculiar orange (which was very popular back then). They were also wealthier and wore expensive beaded gowns. Their wealth also afforded them more hairspray and electrical tape to hold all the right parts in all the right places. Seriously, this was a thing in the 1990s. I didn't plan to win it but coming in runner-up brought home the money too. So I happened to win and now was my time to follow in the footsteps of all the women before me, with whom I shared nothing in common.

PUBLIC HUMILIATION

So the council meeting was finally wrapping up, the reporters left and there were a lot of unhappy politicians in the room. Their grumpiness was obvious. I figured I'd take them out of their misery by speaking for 2-3 minutes so we could all go home and get on with life.

The Mayor of Cleveland announced me and called me to the podium. He said with a chuckle, "She's from Mansfield, let's give her a welcome anyway." You can joke about a lot of things but my hometown isn't one of them. That is where I earned my stripes. It was a hard place. It taught me a lot. While I'm sure the mayor was joking, I didn't like it much.

I leaned into the microphone and thanked the mayor and said, "People here in Cleveland always laugh at me when I tell them I'm from Mansfield and they always bring up the big prison there," and before I knew it I said it, "Well, most of the people in the prison are from Cleveland anyway, so what does that tell you?"

Damn.

A roar filled the air! It was a mixture of laughs and unapproving groans. The response was so loud that it apparently awakened me from my unconscious self. I looked around at a few disappointed faces and quickly said, "I'm just kidding." No one heard me though. I said a few words of thanks, tucked my tail and got the hell out of there.

A PERSONAL SMEAR CAMPAIGN

Later that night my mom called. "Quick, turn on the news, you're on it!" This was before my broadcasting days and before social media but not before remotes. I frantically searched through my comforter for my remote. I clicked on the channel and there I was wearing that tacky sash making a cruel remark about residents of the city I was trying to win over. It turns out there was one lone reporter and his loyal cameraman in the back of that boring meeting, rolling on my every word.

I was so ashamed. But it didn't stop there.

The next morning, I became the topic of a few talk radio programs. "She's no diplomat, that's for sure," one guy said. "I can't believe she said that! What a stupid thing to say," another woman chimed in. Actually what she said was pretty stupid too, but it was time to beat up on me, the Miss Ohio beauty queen who blasted the mayor at his own meeting. Finally, another guy chimed in and said, "Give the girl a break, it's not big deal and she's probably right, most of the inmates in that Mansfield prison are probably from Cleveland." Then a reporter chimed in and told the actual inmate population stats.

It was humiliating. I felt a deep sense of shame. I'm smarter than that, I thought. Aren't I? Some people had their own spin on it, calling out beauty over brains. It ticked me off because no one knew or even inquired about me or my platform. They were judging me over a 15-second slip of the tongue.

I could have allowed anger to be the dominant emotion in this situation but instead, shame crashed my party.

THE RESIDUE OF SHAME

It caused distractions. I was more careful when speaking in public, which prevented me from allowing my true self to shine through. I overanalyzed every situation and response. There was a serious game of head trash building up. My head was so full, it locked out the good stuff. I was stuck on shame.

It wasn't until I made it to the international Miss World competition that I realized I was being terribly hard on myself. I observed some of the most beautiful women berating themselves, and crying uncontrollably over ridiculous stuff. It was mind blowing. That experience taught me to go easy, and be more gentle with myself.

Everyone makes mistakes. You might not speak it into a microphone on a public forum but you'll mess up. When things go wrong you must get it out of your system. Resist the urge to block feeling anything. You are human. Shame stagnates us. Shame is a manufactured emotion driven by bad circumstances. Choose a better, more empowered way to feel.

ENOUGHNESS TOOL #10:
TAMING YOUR SELF LOATHING

1. Replace the Emotion: Sadness is more fluid. We can move more easily through feelings of sadness instead of shame. When you talk about sadness, you get a very different response from people. They react differently to sadness. It brings compassion and breathing room, whereas shame often brings pity. No one wants to be in a pity party with you. You would never want your nine-year-old self to be ashamed of who she is, what she did or what she thought. Don't do it to your 29- or 49- or 79-year-old self.

2. Give Yourself Permission: When you find yourself making mistakes or hurt by life's battles, grant supreme permission to be sad or angry or feel grief. These emotions are easier to feel. They are less berating or belittling. You have to feel something. It is how we are wired, but don't engage in shamefulness. I've eliminated the word from my vocabulary, and you should too.

3. Trust that You Have Everything You Need: Everything that you need to address shame or blame is built in to your Enoughness. Some days you might need to dig a little deeper to connect to it but it is right there. It is as close as your breath. When you feel winded open your bag and allow your fingers to find their way through the compartments. Take time to hold the work you are doing close to your heart. Know that you are stronger than shame, you can overcome the obstacle that causes feelings of self loathing.

You can run but you can't hide.

YOUR PERSONAL MASK

As humans, we are good at preventing others from seeing who we really are. We have our disguises intact. It might feel better to hide behind something that keeps the world from seeing who we truly are. It might feel OK to protect ourselves and prevent others from figuring us out.

In reality, playing any role other than your authentic self is exhausting. It tires you out. You have to remember the disguise that you are selling, all of the stories, details and background. You basically are lying to yourself and others. And those lies are loaded with fatigue and frustration because the upkeep is exhausting. You must remember the lies so you don't reveal them. You also must remember the truth, so you don't reveal it either. Whew! That's a lot of remembering.

When we hide, we cut off a lifeline. We disengage from life. We cut away nurturing relationships and skirt around accountability. Our values weaken and boundaries get crossed. We shut out the source of life when we are disingenuous. A calamity happens but we think it is happening because everyone is after us or it is our signature bad luck or the world has suddenly turned on us. No, we've turned on ourselves.

HIDING IN PLAIN SIGHT

Ms Beulah was hiding in our dining room. That limelight consisted of a very comfortable and predictable setting. From the corner down the street to the walk through our front door right over to the piano bench, she was bathed in comfort.

She knew the routine. She had a familiar audience, she was safe from rejection and ridicule. Her mask was rigidly affixed. New people and opportunities could not break through it.

Beulah, like so many of us, can hide in plain sight. Most of us have never been on the brink of a possible Motown record deal but we've had some entertaining offers come our way. Like many people, I have curled up a time or two and backed away. Leaving a box, possibly a gift, forever unopened.

To come out of the shadows, you have to come clean and show up in your real suit of armor. This means being vulnerable. Showing vulnerability isn't a sign of weakness. It is actually a sign of courage. You have to give in to whatever scares you about being the real you.

Retreating costs a lot. Don't pay the price.

Beulah paid a hell of a high price. Whenever I think of her I wonder what might have happened if she took off her mask. What could her life look like if she could let go of that fear and her fixed way of being? What else could she have accomplished? What if she stepped out of the box just one time? Maybe her entire world would be changed for the better. We will never know.

It takes as much work to hide behind our junk as it does to come clean and live a life out in the light. Hiding behind the stories we've told ourselves about habitual cycles or misgivings is counterproductive. Making a choice to be real and get to the root of who you really are cracks all false foundations. Being real means being great at who you really are instead of some version of what others want or expect you to be.

BEWARE OF THE THICKENING AGENT

When you are working to make yourself whole, you will begin to notice strange things happening around you. You will pick up on pretentious people more quickly than before. You will take notice of artificial ingredients in your life.

Among those artificial things is mascara commercials. They sell thicker, longer, healthier lashes while the model is wearing fake lashes.

So the message is my lashes will look like hers if I buy the product. The hidden message is never revealed unless you are reading between the lines or lashes. It's an unrealistic expectation and it goes far back to before you and I were born.

Our parents were conditioned with boys wearing blue and girls wearing pink. The marketing campaign was so effective that people still buy into it today, staying true to the trend. Following trends can drag us away from our true selves. Trends hold our voice captive.

The opposite of hiding is revealing. Reveal your true self. Get real about using the tools in this book. Foster your Enoughness by putting the advice in this book into action.

ENOUGHNESS TOOL #11:
GET READY FOR THE BIG REVEAL

1. Stop Over-Apologizing: We say "I'm sorry" over trivial things. Sorry, I didn't hear you, sorry I don't have a pen, sorry the sun isn't shining today. Leave apologies for sincere oversights. Repeating the phrase "I'm sorry" starts to stick in our psyche. We actually start to believe that we are, in fact, sorry. The word attaches itself to negative emotions that leave us empty.

2. Look People in the Eye: Start this today. Lock your eyes with people you are talking with and listen with your eyes. The more you do it the more comfortable it gets. Don't worry about what he or she is thinking, just do your part and honor them through direct eye contact.

3. Look Yourself in the Eye: For the next week any time you pass a mirror look into your eyes before noticing your great pantsuit or killer pumps. Let the material things come second to this honorable exercise. As you stare into your own eyes, remind yourself of your greatness, rekindle past victories, allow yourself to be proud of the woman staring back at you.

4. Commit to Something that Challenges your Authenticity: Kids are great for this. They generally are straight shooters like Mama Eatmon. They cut to the chase and tell us the truth. Carve out some time and put yourself out there with your family or colleagues. Let your true self come through. Let every word and mannerism reveal your most genuine self. If something feels fake and forced, stop. Wait until the impulse inspires you because that's what you want to move on.

If you're going to do it, transcend your effort.
Step to it, fully. Sluggish attempts define your brand
just as quickly as massive action.

PERSONAL BRANDING

You can't persuade others to believe or invest in your brand if you lack the ability to know who you are and why you are doing what you're doing. Falling short on these two answers leads to misinterpretations which gets in the way of success. If you are lacking, your brand is lacking and prospects will notice.

Making the transition from television news into entrepreneurship was especially challenging in terms of building my personal brand. I no longer had access to the CBS marketing and advertising team piecing together promos. When I launched my business, I instantly became my own promoter. This wasn't necessarily my wheelhouse but I had to figure it out in order to grow the business, make money and hire marketing experts later on down the road.

The "figuring it out" part was a significant learning curve. I call it beautiful trouble. While I was enjoying the opportunity to own a business I was selling myself short by building a brand that wasn't a true reflection of myself. When I met with potential partners or sponsors they often seemed confused, asking, "So what do you do again?" The time I spent explaining the actual vision was eating up the clock and getting me nowhere.

TURN DOWN THE NOISE

There was so much noise in my mind that I was confused about my brand. It seemed everywhere I looked from a TV commercial, to a magazine ad, to a story on my newsfeed, someone was telling me how to think about myself. My electronic mailbox was receiving notes from "abandoned women" in Africa claiming that if I were a good person, I'd help them out in return for $40k. The physical mailbox was just as bad with advertisements about miracle wrinkle cream and how much better I'd feel if I saw a plastic surgeon. I turned it all off and started researching. I began researching myself.

The first thing I did was take a huge sheet of paper, tack it to the wall in my office, and starting writing down every single job I had. I started with my first gig as a janitorial assistant, then Pizza Hut waitress and all the way through my journalism career. From there I began pulling out important aspects from each position to identify the skills I learned and strengths I built in each job.

I used those answers as a foundation to my consulting work. I was strong in communications and media. I was also a proficient public speaker and I was studying social media. These became the four pillars of the first phase of my business. That was the easy part.

YOUR SIGNATURE STYLE

I found many other women, equally or more qualified, traveling the same road as me. There is always competition and I had to push my way into the sandbox to play. This is where the real branding was born. Figuring out what makes you different and, even more important, who is going to care. Those two questions led me to a signature style of personal branding.

It was those two questions that steered me away from unintentionally copying a brand or trying to do what is popular in the moment. It is an interesting mix because while you're aware of your competitors, some of them soaring to success while you're just coming out of the gate, you have to examine yourself and make sure you are not falling prey to the shiny stuff.

Perfecting my brand has opened doors for me to work with some of the leading companies in the world such as KeyBank, Sherwin-Williams,

Cleveland Clinic and others. By defining my personal message, networking became simple. I was attracting people who had a direct interest in my services.

The word was getting out and now good news began filling my inboxes with requests to consult with companies and organizations on the four pillars. Then a fifth subject entered my repertoire: Personal Branding. I was thrilled to share insights on authentic branding with women at YWCA, Swagelok and other organizations.

BRANDING DRILL

Humans are predictable. Advertising agencies have that predictability nailed down to a science. They know our pain points and how to relate to our emotions. Here's a quick drill to show you just how effective they are at marketing to our emotions:

How do you spell Relief?
Don't squeeze the _____.
Maybe she's born with it, may it's _____.
It keeps going and going and going.

Chances are you could finish most of these one-liners because our minds have been conditioned to buy these products. We believe they will somehow make us better or make us feel better. The message is emotionally appealing.

What's your one-liner?

Treat your personal brand the same way. Appeal to the emotions. Help people buy in to your ideals and goals.

CURRENT BEHAVIOR AND INNER MOTIVATION

You can build a genuine, reputable brand through a unique look at personal potential, authenticity and ultimate goals. By cross referencing your current behavior with inner motivation you'll gain insight into relevant brand-building knowledge.

Every day you must promote your brand. Regardless of whether it's intentional or not, you are creating a reputation. To establish a personal brand, there are five traits that, when applied correctly, can transform your message. The following traits are collected from real-life interactions.

ENOUGHNESS TOOL #12:
BUILD AN EMPOWERING BRAND

What do you want people to believe about you? What do you want them to say? Everything counts. From your workplace environment to your colleagues' and clients' perceptions about you, it's all fair game. What you leave for others to decide can hinder your progress. Take control of your brand and your future.

1. How Do You Make Others Feel? What impressions do you leave behind? Do people want to know more about you?

2. What Are Your Strengths? Are others aware of them or are they hidden? Do the same exercise I did. Make columns on notebook paper to list your work history and skills. Also, ask others to weigh in on identifying a strength marker. They may recognize something that you haven't considered.

3. How Do You Build Relationships? How do you impact others? Later in the book, we'll delve into more relationship advice, but for now, observe how you impact others.

4. How Do You Tell Your Story? It's your story and you are the author. Tell it from an empowering stance. If you've had a troubled past or are experiencing hard times, be careful how you share your story. People don't want to feel pity, they want to feel empowered. Empower them.

5. What Do People Say About You When You Leave the Room? Have you ever wondered what they're saying when you exit? Don't wonder. Tell them what to say by how you treat them. Reread #1. Help people feel inspired, empowered, excited and validated through your personal brand.

Carry Your Zen With You

PART THREE: BE WHOLE

In a world filled with annoyances, we're finding virtual pop-up ads in real life too. The distractions from the email dings and newsfeed alerts pull on our attention. Our energy is depleted by a long list of to-do's which we try to micromanage. Miniature tasks quickly grow into mountains of problems. We can't focus. We need help staying awake and help falling asleep.

We're in a hurry to get there and finish up. We eat on the go. We're pushing time away.

We're doing more work but we're not getting more time.

We're grinding ourselves to a pulp, unable to enjoy the process of the journey.

Leslie was on an incredible journey. She made her way into a top executive position at a multi-million dollar company, managing over 1500 people. She was leading by leaps and bounds. At the time, the 60-year-old was the only woman in the C-suite.

PANIC ATTACKS

One day she confided in me that before the board meetings she would go into the bathroom and have major panic attacks. "I couldn't understand why I was so out of control," she shared with me. Leslie tried to make sense of it all but the attacks continued. She found herself putting on artificial armor when sitting with the guys. This caused a crack in her wholeness.

Another example of being separated from self is Mary, a 20-something secretary whom I met at a networking event. She attempted to manage a new job, finish college, move into a new apartment and deal with a nasty break-up from her boyfriend. This attractive woman who looked like the picture of health at 25 had a massive stroke.

Both women sought medical advice and while they vastly differ in age they were essentially told the same thing: You have to take better care of yourself. Each followed a regimen of exercise, healthier foods and stress-busting tools. But taking better care of yourself extends far beyond the basics of food and exercise. That is a great place to begin but there is more to it.

YOU ARE THE GATHERER

Taking better care of ourselves is about getting whole. Getting to wholeness is getting to completion. It is a balancing act of sorts. You are balancing the many parts of yourself; your Worth and Wisdom compartments. You are a gatherer. You snap all the pieces together and allow them to help you navigate and progress through life.

You must monitor the process. You are the observer of your inner power and outer being. You are the controller of the energy you share with others and what you allow into your body. You are the master of your thoughts. You are the master over all of this.

Right before your flight takes off you can sometimes see the workers on the tarmac tossing bags into the belly of the airplane. You notice big, overstuffed bags, some with holes, others missing a wheel or handles. You see it all. The owners of these bags might have everything stuffed inside the luggage but for some reason it's become unraveled. It's mangled and stretched. This is how we are when Wholeness has exited our lives.

LOOKING GOOD ON PAPER

Things look good on paper. You are hearing the cha-chings in your bank account. You are having a ball in Rome (the one in Italy or Ohio) with girlfriends but you are becoming unhinged. You are frazzled and tired. When you are standing at the baggage claim, waiting for your Enoughness bag, you can easily see who has it together and who does not.

That is how it looked to me when I hit my downward spiral. My bag was definitely mangled and unrecognizable. Parts of my life were shattered as opposed to whole.

My mind, body and spirit had no unity. My mind grappled with confusion while my body felt fatigue and my spirit seemed dormant. Hitting financial hardships after walking away from a high-paying, high-profile position was more than tough. It was hell. Darkness was aggressively filling in throughout my life. The more positive I tried to be, the harder I fell into ruin.

I went from earning a six-figure income, more money than anyone in my family had ever seen, to needing assistance from the government.

I always prided myself on taking care of myself. It was a promise I made to myself as a little girl after watching some of my relatives mismanage funds and hit hard times. I didn't want to repeat the cycle. Even when I got married, I didn't rely on my husband to take care of me; that was my job. I was an able-bodied smart woman. I could handle it. Until one day when I couldn't handle it, I repeated the same cycle.

Looking back on the time when I thought I was winning, I wasn't being transparent with myself. I wasn't truly living the life I yearned for. I wasn't living, period. I had no fire in my belly or song in my heart but I looked the part. I was covered up in nice clothes, a nice car and a chic downtown townhome. Those were material possessions, things that can easily become obsessions. They did nothing to help bridge the divide between myself and the wholeness I knew I was destined to have.

Stuff and big beautiful cars will never be the pathway to finding wholeness. They only cushion the ride.

PAUSE TO KEEP GOING

Being whole is absolutely necessary. It is the glue to the Be Worthy and Be Wise compartments binding everything together. When one area is in trouble, your wholeness is the rescuer. Another way to look at it is when you're exercising one area of the body, the instructor will remind you to relax other parts. For example, while toning your stomach muscles with sit-ups, you might automatically tighten the back of your neck.

Fitness trainers will tell you to pause from that exercise and stretch out the other area you are tightening. The same is true while filling your bag. We get so caught up in the pursuit we neglect the pieces that help us get to the finish line.

You can't get to your desired finish line without wholeness. It is simply not possible.

SOFTENING HEARTS

Being whole means nothing is omitted. It is the entirety, the totality of you. It is everything about you all wrapped up into the pristine promise of everything good, everything right. It's well-being and being true to yourself and others. It is knowing who you are and what you stand for.

The Free Dictionary defines whole as containing all components; complete. Not divided or disjoined. A Biblical definition says that it is the state of being perfectly well in body, soul and spirit. It is complete sanctification and restoration.

In some instances the words holiness and healing have been paired with wholeness and rightfully so. Your completeness is all encompassing.

This is the final compartment in your Enoughness bag. It completes you. I designed the next session to supplement every aspect of you. Use the sections to adjust your ability to honor self-care. Use it to soften and strengthen your heart. Use it to help soften the hearts of other people. Use it to align or realign yourself with all of the immaculate things that create harmony with each piece and peace of yourself.

Settle in.

This is a safe place. Wrap yourself in a blanket of certainty. Be confident that the tools you need are here and ready for you.

Joy is being in a state of wonder and collecting
feel-good moments along the way.

JOYFUL LIVING

You are not laughing enough. Not even close to enough.
Kids are kicking our butts on this one. On average, most four-year-olds have laugh ripples in their bellies about 300 times a day. A 40-year-old? Try 296 times less per day!

Why are we so uptight, or as my great grandmother would say, why are our panties in such a bunch?

This is no laughing matter. If you prohibit joy from rolling into your life, you are interfering with your health and emotional well-being. I don't care how much work went in to the other compartments of your Enoughness bag, if you are unhealthy, none of it matters because you won't have the strength to persevere.

JOY CAN'T BREATHE

If you're glued to news on television and in your newsfeeds, things might look bleak. Many news outlets will destroy whatever hopefulness you have. Hopelessness smothers joyfulness.

Every time I click on my social media feed, someone is facing death and destruction. Good news is hard to find. We have to seek it out. Our lives depend on it.

Some relatives and colleagues might add to the bad news bucket, tossing in their daily gossip, lonely hearts from old breakups and Go Fund Me accounts for broken knees. People have problems. We all do. But you can't let their problems steal your joy. Their stuff can't rock your boat. You have to keep rowing. You have to keep going.

Have you noticed how so many TV commercials sell you drugs for this ailment or that illness? Some people need medicine. But there is an additional supplement missing. You've heard the saying that laughter is the best medicine. Let's try it out.

VITALITY IS VITAL

Turning on your funny bone can reduce stress. Psychologists and healthcare professionals agree that good old-fashioned laughter reduces stress hormones such as cortisol, epinephrine and dopamine. It can enhance the good hormones. A silly roar can increase your heart health in many ways as well.

Bringing bliss into each day of our lives is critical for our health. Vitality is critical in creating a life of value. Feeling good should be a goal that we all aim for. Turning up the corners of your mouth is an easy step. Step it up.

I have a confession to make. When I am home alone I pump up some music, usually something by Michael Jackson or the song "September" by Earth, Wind & Fire and I go! I dance! It's not just the two-step either, it is a full-out marathon. I'm singing the words, snapping my fingers and swaying which ever way my body decides to move. This almost instantly alerts my feel-good emotions.

The songs themselves send me down memory lane, recalling good times with family and friends. It takes me back to a simpler time when my relatives were young, healthy and vibrant. They danced. There were lots of dances in our living room as music poured through the floor model record player. The women were always in the kitchen prepping food. In the moment of my personal disco fever, I can smell the aroma of those amazing meals.

All of this pours into my 5-10 minute dance. I walk away a little sweaty but I'm beaming with joy. The trip down memory lane gives me comfort and the dancing makes me happy.

The treasures of joyfulness can be found in something small and seemingly insignificant. You never know what will trigger it but when it hits you just go with it.

WHEN JOYFUL BUBBLES POP

Uncertain and sad times squeeze the air out of joy bubbles. The air evaporates and flattens our fun. But even in times like these you can focus on something that triggers goodness and reminds you that not all is lost.

Shortly after 9-11 when the country was in a very somber mood I was in the airport in Dallas, waiting in the long security line. No one had anything to smile about. Everyone was dealing with the business of stripping down to the essentials and following the new protocol.

The tight security was new for everyone, travelers and TSA agents alike. Everyone seemed patient until the small, docile man in front of me met a large-framed, wide-hipped female security guard at the first checkpoint.

"Sir," she said, "You can't take this on board." She pulled out a large jar of perfumed Chanel body cream. It was wrapped in clear paper with a bow on top.

The man flipped his blond bangs back and looked at the oversized woman. "Say whaaat?" he said in a high-pitched nails-down-the-chalk-board voice. I laughed and thought, oh this is going to be good.

The two of them went back and forth. The young man explained it was a gift for a friend, and he purposely wrapped it in cellophane paper so security could see it. The TSA agent told him, "No can do! No way is this 'ere cream going on that plane!" She smiled a little, as if she knew where this luxurious cream might end up. The guy asked me to watch his roller bag. I agreed. He stomped his little self away for a few minutes.

MILLION DOLLAR CREAM

When I looked up I saw joy illuminating from his face. He was beaming! He was happy and there was a sense of pleasure emanating from his body. The closer he came to the line, the stronger the scent of perfume became. His neck was glistening... a lot. He got back in line, with the jar in hand and handed it to the agent. It was completely empty. Not a drop of cream left.

He layered himself in that expensive cream. All of it! His hands were oily, his elbow looked slippery and the back of his neck was well moisturized. I could tell that the little fella felt amazing! He looked like he had wrapped himself up in million-dollar cream. I, along with other folks in the line, laughed so hard we could hardly get through security with a straight face. The high five he gave me was a bit sticky, reminding me of the girl in junior high who rejected my plea to join her group. But this time it was a cool, well-intended stickiness.

Sometimes that's what we have to do. We have to layer ourselves in thick, rich expensive cream to let joy seep in. We can't let others confiscate it. That cream could be a massage, a yoga session, watching a comedy with your family or a night out with friends at a comedy club. Let joy in.

It's your responsibility to live a luminous life. Open the lid, lather it on and let it filter through the air. Let your joy invigorate yourself and everyone around you. This is the good stuff. Don't waste it.

ENOUGHNESS TOOL #13:
TEN WAYS TO FIND YOUR OWN JOY

1. Ignite Your Giggle Gauge: There are apps to track your sleeping habits, blood pressure, daily steps and more, so build your own pedometer. Let's tally your ability to howl. Play this game: At the beginning of each week, decide how much joy you want in your life that week. This is a big question and your answer should be just as big. Seeing that joyfulness and laughter compliment each other, note how much you want to laugh, how many good times you want to experience in this week. Write down your goal. Example: I want 1000 laughs.

Next, start piling up the things that will get you to your goal. Be intentional. Create a list of feel good items: Funny books, funny people, animal videos on YouTube, prank calls videos on YouTube, getting your parents to FaceTime you, doing yoga with your dog, tickling a baby, tickling a grown-up, etc.

For each belly laugh, you get a point. Track it. At the end of the week (per my example above I should have 1000 points), reward yourself with a treat. Make the treat something that will enliven your funny bone even more. Make your treats joyful treats.

To make your tracking easier, plant a few glass Mason jars (I prefer glass containers so I can see my goals accumulating) and scrap paper in spaces where you spend most of your time; office desk, kitchen, reading room, etc. Each laugh, toss a piece of paper into the jar. At the end of the week, collect the jars and start counting. Ready? Set. Go!

2. Instruct Your Happy Feet: TV shows like American Bandstand and Soul Train used to give us the skinny on the latest dance moves but today Ellen Degeneres reigns as the dancing queen. Follow her footsteps, turn on your favorite jam and let it rip. If you lack rhythm just slide to the right, slide to the left and turn around and repeat. Hell, you can even do the Hokey Pokey, it will suffice. The point is to get moving, produce adrenaline. Let your moves evoke happiness.

3. Take a Creativity Shower: Standing in isolation, feeling the water hit your body and roll down your back is not only relaxing but it can also enhance your creativity which pushes your joyful button. The sound and feeling of water enlivens our senses and if you indulge without distractions (cell phones and loud noises) you can tap into a serenity that might seem more appropriately reserved for meditation or prayer.

In a television interview 10x Grammy Award-winner and master producer behind the hit song "Happy," Pharrell Williams talked to Oprah about his sacred experience in the shower. The artist said some of his best music ideas and lyrics came to him while showering. He attributed this to the "sensory deprivation" that comes from being audibly distracted by running water. Then he allows his mind to wander.

Spend some time away from the world. Ban cell phones and other attention-getting devices. Creating clarity reduces confusion. When we can see clearly, we are refreshed and ready to take action. All of this creates enormous feel-good emotions.

4. Pay For Someone's Lunch Without Getting Credit: I do this a lot at Bob Evans and other restaurants. Ask your server for the check of the table you want to treat, let him or her know you don't want to be identified and secretly pay their tab, then scram. You don't need to see their reaction or receive a "thank you." Knowing that you possibly made someone's day a bit brighter will bring you enormous joy.

5. Take a Tech (and text) Detox: One day per week, turn it all off. Arianna Huffington, the on-line news media mogul, has spoken out a lot about her need to change the way she lived and worked after health issues surfaced. In books, blogs and magazine interviews, Adrianna said one of the things she changed was removing her cell phone from the bedroom at night. That advice comes from a woman who runs a major digital news circuit: Huffington Post.

You need a break. Take one. Set your gadgets off to the side. Rest your fingers from texting and use them to hold hands with your favorite people or braid your hair. Cut out the tweeting and blurt out your feelings over dinner with friends. Stop the LOL'ing and laugh out loud in real time with real people. Try it one day a week and when you fall in love with it, go for more time, maybe the entire weekend.

6. Consume Meals with People You Enjoy: I feel better in good company. Each day, have at least one meal with someone who brings you joy. Make it an occasion instead of gathering around the television to eat. Make sure these people bring cheer into your life. It's been proven that breaking bread with folks you love helps your food digest easier.

7. Learn the Name of Your Server: Each barista, every waiter and waitress deserves your attention. Give it to them. Make your outings lovely and entertaining. Exchange small talk with the people serving you. Get to know them. Don't do it because you fear them slipping a finger in your food. Do it to create authentic delight in both your life and theirs. People in these jobs are always wearing a name tag. Use it. Celebrate them.

8. Use Glass and Recycle Every Chance You Get: We share this planet with each other. We're responsible for its current condition and how we leave it after our time is up. Working to spruce up our world gives us a sense of togetherness, accomplishment and the satisfaction of doing good. Good work contributes to good vibrations. Good vibrations signals our joy meters.

Several reports show that globally, humans purchase a million plastic bottles per minute, and 91% of that plastic is not recycled. It's estimated that by 2050 the ocean will have more plastic by weight than fish. Our seas were not meant to be a dumping site.

When possible, switch to glass. Buy several cotton tote bags for groceries, and forgo the plastic ones. Even collecting your fruits and vegetables with reusable natural produce bags helps. You can pick up a bunch of these at stores like Target. Storing your leftovers in covered glass dishes can not only save on plastic waste but it is healthier to heat up in the microwave.

If you absolutely must use plastic, recycle every single item. No exceptions. Don't contribute to polluting our beautiful planet.

9. Pet the Dog (or Cat): Pets give an enormous amount of joy all by themselves. Cuddle with you four-legged BFF. Medical doctors have noted many times the health benefits we get from our pets including helping reduce stress. If now isn't the time for you to care for a furry friend, visit the animal shelter and spend time with those precious babes. Do it for them and for yourself.

10. Take Ownership (and stock) of Your Body: We accumulate a lot of stuff in life, but bodies aren't one of them. We know we only have this one unit, yet maintaining this vehicle can be a daunting task. It's funny how we prioritize the upkeep of our homes with the right repair when warning signs appear. We rush in to get oil for our cars when the red light blinks but we ignore the warning signs our bodies send us. Too many times, people wait too long to pinpoint a problem in the making. They wait until the tidal wave crashes in and then it can be too late. The damage is done. Nourish your body every single day.

Stay hydrated, drink enough water each day. Eat more dark greens. Find an eating program that invigorates you. Food can make us feel sluggish or absolutely incredible, so find your absolutely incredible. Use your food for vitality. The Mediterranean plan works wonders for me. There are many books and medical articles describing the health benefits of this particular lifestyle. Find what works for you and stick a fork in it.

If your clothes make you feel frumpy, you're frumpy. If your clothes make you feel fabulous, you're fabulous.

Clear Your Closet

Life is uber busy. The busier it gets the more we run. Running and gunning requires fast decision making skills. Your morning routine probably consists of the basics: brushing your teeth, getting dressed while dressing the kids, gulping down some coffee and then you're out the door. You manage to get your shoes on the right feet along with matching socks but does your outfit match the message you want to send to your colleagues and clients?

What are you wearing and why? What message are you sending the world about how you feel about yourself? Are the garments in your closet fueling your life or adding baggage to an already heavy load?

Your Enoughness bag is going to love this.

I had a lot of stuff. About 90% of it didn't hold any significance in my life. My closet was filled with a mixture of old sweatshirts from high school, big, baggy blazers from my TV news days, old purses and a few new contemporary pieces. It was a lot of mix-matched garments from various eras in my life. Because I am a shoe activist, I welcomed many pairs into my closet.

Things were crammed in my closet space but they were also crammed in other physical spaces.

THE BODY IS THE CANVAS

I see my body as a canvas and the clothing as art. The final result should be a reflection of who I am. It should be a statement of the life I am living. In the past, I liked most of the clothing hanging in my closet but

I have to be honest it didn't do anything for me. Some fabrics didn't move or flow. They didn't reflect the energy and zest I felt for life.

Other outfits were too tight. They fit snugly in all the wrong places. Pretty pieces but best suited for another body type. These garments didn't make me smile and I didn't feel extra good in them. Instead they reminded me of the body I once had and I don't need anything distracting me from who I am today.

Being whole is about being Beyond Enough in the now. If your garments don't represent your truth, they need to go.

EDIT YOUR LIFE

When I turned 40 I realized the high school sweatshirts no longer had their rah rah rah appeal, and it was definitely time to graduate them. I ran my fingers through several columns of folded garments and only one piece made me smile. It was a fun knitted dress. Whenever I wore it I felt beautiful. It flowed perfectly around my knees. I pulled that dress out and had a little conversation with it. "Hey girl! Where have you been? Let's have some fun together!" I found happiness in that summer dress.

Around this time my friend Jana sent me a book, The Life-Changing Magic of Tidying Up: The Japanese art of decluttering and organizing. The author, Marie Kondo, solidified my action of touching clothes and keeping what "sparks joy" and discarding the other pieces.

Marie, a Japanese cleaning consultant, has a simple system for decluttering your home. Her step-by-step approach helps you relate to everything in your living space. Once you examine the things that are in your home from a 'what brings you joy' perspective, you'll see that more than likely you're surrounded by a lot of stuff that does just the opposite.

I began searching for more joyfulness in my closet and the end result was alarming. Ten mid-sized trash bags filled with clothes that were in good to excellent condition but they just didn't produce what I needed. I donated them to Salvation Army and shared some cute outfits with a fitness trainer at my gym.

CLEARING CLUTTER CREATES OPPORTUNITY

When I got rid of the extra clothes I found plenty of space in my closet. But something more extraordinary happened. I began closing more deals and received unexpected work for my consulting business. Clearing out our physical spaces creates room for new things. Those things can be physical or otherwise.

I was so inspired by this new action that I started clearing drawers and cupboards. My actions inspired my husband to clean the garage and while he was finishing the two-day job he received a phone call. The deal that had been on the blink for months was now closed. I stood in the doorway and watched his eyes widen as if he had seen a ghost. This stuff works!

We can't control what happens in the world but we can control what we bring into our homes and why. Our homes should include items that we adore, things that complement us. Here are four ways to get started.

ENOUGHNESS TOOL #14: FOUR WAYS
TO WHITTLE DOWN TO THE ESSENTIALS

1. Rid the Clutter: Take a trip through the closet and drawers and connect with your clothing. Find what reaches your happy spot and what makes you feel frumpy and lackluster. You know what to do next: give it away or trash it. Don't hang on to it. Make room for the next big thing (both physical and emotional).

2. Know the Message You Want to Send: Decide on your personal message you want to share with colleagues and clients. Do you want them to see a well put together look or a haggard, "I just threw something on…again" look? We are judged by our appearance. Make sure you're getting the verdict you desire.

3. Build a Classic Uniform: Since you're not a supermodel yet, invest in a few classic pieces that you can wear interchangeably with outfits. Start with classic trousers that complement your body frame, a pair that makes you walk and talk like the boss that you are. Invest in your confidence.

When I first started in TV news, I didn't have money for clothing but I wanted to present myself as a well put together professional. With my first paycheck I went in to Stein Mart, an American discount department store, with a short list and a coupon. I walked out with two pairs of pants, black and khaki, a black dress with a matching blazer, a navy skirt and four shirts (two solids and two prints). I borrowed some of my mother's jewelry. For six months I made this uniform work in conjunction with a few additional suits I already owned. It worked well and it got the job done.

4. Just Because it's On Sale Doesn't Mean that it Should Be On You: Other trinkets and stuff we find on sale might better suit someone else. Stop buying it. If it doesn't make you sparkle, leave it.

Longhand requires stillness of the mind, body and heart.
You are giving a lot of yourself in that moment.
Pass the stillness on to others.

WRITE LETTERS

We don't write it down anymore. Our feelings are typed out in a quick email. Our grocery lists are packed away in a neat app. Our to-do list is brilliantly organized in a color-coded spreadsheet. We don't cross our own T's or dot our own I's. We're clicking it all away.

We are literally losing touch.

Non-stop connections to our electronic devices can leave us feeling quirky, a bit fidgety at times. There is a quiet rush to it all. We type fast, click through dozens of documents within seconds while responding to those quick emails. Everything is mechanical. We are heavily invested in this way of working, and for some of us playing. We have emotional investments in this as well.

Pecking out a comment on a friend's uplifting post can bring a sensation of joy but how long does it last? Responding to a grieving classmate on Twitter might generate feelings of sadness but how long do you sympathize? Our emotions are moving just as quickly as our actions.

We are disconnecting.

HBR
On my FaceBook timeline I don't have my birthday listed on the page. I'm not hiding my age, it's because most of the birthday wishes seem robotic. "HBR" (Happy Birthday Raquel) is so trite. For goodness sakes, we can't even type out the words any more! How much more

time does it actually take to type out the phrase? This is nonsense.

Young people are handing in homework like this. Some of them are speaking like this. During the holidays, gathered around the table a relative cracked a hilarious joke and my teenage cousin was the only one not laughing. Instead he said "LOL" several times. Nothing can replace a good hearty laugh.

We're losing touch with our feelings, and letter-writing can help guide us back to our center.

LETTERS WITH MILEAGE

My letter-writing practice began during junior high when I found a pen pal through a kids' magazine. It was so exciting to exchange notes with other kids whom I had not met. Each month I received a letter in the mail. Yay! While the adults in the house were getting bills, I was getting personal messages from a kid in Iowa or California. I was just as eager to respond.

Today, my pen pal writing continues. One of my dearest friends, Jana, lives in San Francisco. We can't easily hook up for Sunday brunch or a trip to the mall. There are 2,459 miles between us but that's nothing that a 47-cent postage stamp can't conquer.

We don't do much emailing or texting either. Instead we rely on phone calls and spontaneous notes and letters. We invest heavily in stationery.

Receiving Jana's letters creates a tidal wave of feelings. The moment I see her handwriting, I feel that same sensation I did as a kid. I know it's something personal and it's something good for me. Her letters brighten the flow of news and bills falling through my mail chute.

I relish reading her words. I make this time special, sitting in a comfy spot, sipping on hot tea and doing nothing else but reading a note from my dear friend. I can actually hear her voice in my head as I read it. Her words remind me of the friendship we've cultivated and I'm deeply proud of that.

I continue to write letters to my husband and I have a box of love letters he has written to me. They outshine greeting cards because they are his genuine words, his real feelings. They are a pure part of him expressed through his unique penmanship. The special words of endearment he addresses to me are personal, lovely and priceless.

LETTERS WITH PURPOSE

When I was 39, I asked ten women in my life who were all over the age of 40 to write me a letter. Their instructions were simple: What do you wish you had known at 40? I asked them to gift me the letter for my 40th birthday.

The women wrote their thoughts, wishes and advice in longhand and mailed them to me. I collected them all in a beautiful box until my birthday. The box was the first thing I opened on the morning of my big 4-0.

It was an emotionally charged experience. I laughed, I cried, I gasped with excitement and felt empathy for some of them. I was so honored to feel it all and read it all. There I was in my living room sipping tea as the morning June sun hit my face, holding precious words of wisdom from women I loved and respected. It was a supreme moment. What a truly beautiful gift in the artform of handwritten letters. Those letters made an indelible impact on my life.

FRIENDSHIP FRIDAYS

Don't let all the communications in your relationships arrive by email and texts. On some Fridays I go into a ceremonial bliss of letter-writing. I call it Friendship Friday. I grab my favorite stationery and write a letter or expression of gratitude to a friend.

I view penmanship as a form of art. It is a firsthand account of my experiences that I wish to share. I don't put every detail of my life out there on social media. There are things I withhold to share in my more intimate circle. Writing it down is genuine and therapeutic.

Friendship Friday slows me down. It puts me in touch with myself and the addressee. You can indulge in this quiet space too. It will calm the chaos of beeps and chirps from your gadgety home or office.

Handwritten letters are comforting. Psychologists and medical doctors agree that letter writing is a positive activity with many great benefits. It challenges your penmanship and it keeps your brain sharp. There is no automatic spell check or other red-line attention getters. It's just you, the paper and the pen.

There is something about putting the pen to paper and crafting words that captures your feelings. These words helps the recipient relate to you. Everything from the color of ink you use to the type of paper you choose has meaning in the art of letter-writing. It's your personal expression. It's your personal experience.

ENOUGHNESS TOOL #15:
SIX TYPES OF LETTERS TO WRITE RIGHT NOW
1. Write a Letter to a Child: There are lots of cool kids in the world. Let them know it. For younger kids, print your words. Express your fondness for their coolness. Help frightened children feel safe, help hopeless children see a brighter world.
You have tremendous power behind the stroke of a pen. Use it.

2. Letters to Hurting People: Sometimes you can do little to help others feel better. They may have to strengthen over time. In the meantime, you can remind them of their importance in the world and shed light on their strengths. Use your penmanship as a glimmer of hope.

3. Letters of Gratitude: Thank people for making a positive impact in your life. During my 20s I wrote my grandmother a letter of gratitude, thanking her for making a contribution to my life. When I visited her home a few months later, my heart melted after seeing the letter in a frame in her bedroom.

4. Letters to Your Younger Self: Writing to yourself is a powerful way to connect with your Enoughness. Your letter could be a note of pride, recalling the hardships you have overcome or perhaps it's a note of forgiveness. Write it down and keep it in a safe, sacred place.

5. Letters to Your Older Self: What do you want to do with the rest of your life? How do you want to live? Craft a wish letter to the older, wiser you. List your dreams and goals. Write about how life feels for you right now and what you're hopeful about for the future. I have a letter sealed to my 60-year-old self and apparently I'm still wearing leather leggings. Again, write it down and keep it in a safe, sacred place.

6. Love Letters: Remember this story: Do you like me: Check yes or no? Boys went straight to the point on this one. Instead of following their lead, take your letter into the depths of your soul. Share with your partner, sibling, best friend or parent why you love them and how their love brings value to your life. Don't save any of these words for a eulogy. They won't mean anything to them then. Do it now.

If not now, then when? If not you, then who?

Servant Leadership

The world is full of takers. Some people are all about self. They don't understand or are not interested in the development of others. They are missing an important ingredient in their secret sauce: helping others. This might be challenging, especially if you're wrapped up in trying to get yourself together. You might be bogged down with a hefty to-do list that keeps growing. You might be working on your own personal and professional advancement which can lead you to question your ability to help others. This, my dear friend, is exactly when you need to include others.

We're always trying to fix something about ourselves. Once the adjustment is made, another esteem screw pops loose. Giving yourself permission to help others will refocus you on what's really important. All of that busy work and self-talk can take a back seat.

You have to help others…now.

GET TO WORK!
Sister Rosemary Nyirumbe challenged me and the women at one of my conferences. I asked her: "What can one person do to make a difference?" She responded quickly with, "Plenty, let's get to work!"

I invited Sister Rosemary to Cleveland to keynote at Woman of Power in 2017. Her hard work rescuing girls from human trafficking in Gulu, Uganda has captivated the world. She is one of Time Magazine's Most Influential People in the World. She was also nominated for the Nobel Peace Prize.

Originally, the Ugandan nun wasn't thinking of helping girls until she learned about the problem. Sister Rosemary spun into action when she got news about the terrifying ordeal many young women were facing. She led the Saint Monica's Girls' Vocational School in Gulu, and began teaching the girls how to become self-sufficient.

PURPOSEFUL PURSES

Without a lot of resources to pay for the school, Sister Rosemary needed help. She had one sewing machine and a big idea. She taught the girls how to sew, and within a short period of time they began making beautiful purses out of pop tops, thread and tightly woven rope. The bags continue selling well all over the world.

My reason for bringing this incredible humanitarian to Cleveland wasn't just to instill hope and faith in attendees. It was part of my servant leadership to my own community: To address human trafficking. At the time, Ohio ranked fourth in the country for human trafficking cases.

As a result of Sister Rosemary's brief time with the group, some students from Case Western Reserve University contacted me about their newfound interest in and support for social change and social justice issues. Others began donating to causes to help girls and women affected by human sex trafficking. Everyone was affected. They became more aware of the horrible acts happening in and around their communities. We spread awareness along with a call to action: We can do plenty, get busy!

IT'S CONTAGIOUS

Her visit taught me how much people do care. Bringing Sister Rosemary into the States was costly. It was well over my budget. I went to individual women and asked for contributions to bring the nun to Cleveland. Some couldn't do it but some did. Together, through individual donations and sponsorships, we did it!

When I finally met Sister Rosemary in the hotel lobby she was beaming with joy, pulling her own Enoughness bag. She hugged me tightly and I returned the embrace. When she opened her bag it was loaded with the handmade bags sewn by her students. She had one tiny compartment that held a change of clothes. Ninety-nine point nine percent of the space was dedicated to the mission of helping her girls.

CONTAGIOUS ENERGY

Sister Rosemary is empowered by serving the girls at Saint Monica's. It is her life's work. Sharing ways to help others live an empowered life adds incredible value to your own. Part of being Beyond Enough is pouring into others, enriching their lives. You have opportunities right now to become a servant leader.

When I interviewed KeyBank's Chief of Staff, Trina Evans, at the 2018 Woman of Power Conference, Trina shared great advice on how helping others strengthens our own leadership traits. She leads a staff of several thousand, and her style of leadership is rooted in being authentic and making sure others have what they need to succeed. She is a giver.

PHILANTHROPY

Fashion icon Diane von Furstenberg changed the fashion world when she invented the wrap dress in 1974. She changed the way women dressed. Today she is changing the world in a different way: Philanthropy.

I met Diane in Boston after her keynote speech at Simmons Leadership Conference where she told the audience of 3,500 women how to pay it forward. During our short but meaningful exchange, I thanked her for inspiring me and many other women. She gently grabbed my hands and held them. She looked me in the eye and softly said, "Thank you, tell me more about you."

I spoke about my work and commitment to women's empowerment. She thanked me and shared some stories of determination. She encouraged me to stay on track with my work and continue helping others.

Diane's charitable giving is empowering communities and changing the world. Her foundation supports funds for education, health, human rights, environment, public spaces and the arts. She is a servant leader with a strong desire to transform the lives of others.

The energy that comes from this type of giving, support, volunteering, mentorship, sponsorship and advocacy is contagious. Everyone wins. Here are a few ways you can increase your level of in-kind, selfless giving.

ENOUGHNESS TOOL #16:
WAYS TO BOOST YOUR STEWARDSHIP:

1. Be Selfless: Take an intentional break from your self-interest. Each day, find some time to focus your attention on caring for others. Use your influence skills to impact someone each day. Arrange meetings with newcomers and help them iron out any kinks. Give more time to your mentee. Stay on point with follow-ups and follow-throughs.

2. Serve Followers: Provide a positive outlook for members on your team that might do repetitive tasks or a job that doesn't receive a lot of attention. Help them grow as individuals. Help them start to fill their own Enoughness bag.

3. Meet People Where They Are: Don't try to change people. Don't judge his or her reality. Just be with it. Buckle down and get to know the person or group you are working with. Intensify the sense of community by activating your people skills.

4. Motivate others: When you are directing others to act, don't just tell them what to do. Have a dialogue on why it's a good idea. Exchange thoughts on the benefits of creating a plan to serve others and help communities. Allow the motivation to come from them, not you.

5. Value Communities: Pay special attention to less fortunate members in the community. Remember that your point of view may be vastly different from theirs. That's OK. Use your Emotional Intelligence skills to communicate successfully. The only thing that separates us from other communities is the road we travel to get here. We are all connected, no matter our differences.

If you can't applaud the people in your life, if they are undeserving of your standing ovation, you are pulling dead weight.

RELATIONSHIPS

We are constantly exchanging energy. Both good and bad energy. The people in our inner circle and those closest to us are receivers, carriers and deliverers of this energy. Our lives are woven together. When we are off center, it affects them. The same is true when they are off their game. It triggers an emotional response in us. Relationships thrive or collapse based on how we process and respond to all of this energy and information.

Relationships should be wonderful. They should give us an array of positive emotions and add tremendous value to our lives. They should grant us the freedom to express ourselves. For a lot of people this just isn't the case.

Some people are linked to others because they're lonely or afraid. Some relationships are built on a weak foundation where the needs and wants are based on the wrong things. Bonds like this cause us to break away from self, and we become artificial and weary. We quickly tire from trying to please others. This type of relationship is not nurturing, and friendships can't blossom out of this toxicity.

YOUR FRONT ROW

When you choose to share your life with others, you are extending a personal invitation for them to have a front row seat to your story. They have a ticket to witness your victories and blunders. They have a backstage pass to weather the bumps with you. They should be there to give you a standing ovation; many, many standing ovations.

Oprah Winfrey and Gayle King have this friendship thing down to a science. The two met in 1972 when Oprah was beginning her broadcasting career. They instantly shared commonalities and a friendship quickly took root.

Now after 45 years of friendship Oprah continues to use the same three words when she speaks of Gayle: Trust, love and family.

If you tuned in to the Oprah Winfrey show when it aired on ABC, you watched their friendship play out on cross-country road trips and in enchanting book clubs. Even with TV cameras in their faces, their sisterhood came across as genuine. People at home could relate to the musings of Oprah and Gayle. It reminded them of their own sisterhood. Everything was relatable from the laughing and hushed secrets to the good-spirited questioning of each other's sanity.

TRUST AND LOVE

Both Oprah and Gayle are getting something out of their friendship. Relationships are a give and take. While your moments with close friends aren't being recorded for the world to see, an honest friendship contains a lot of what these two women have displayed: Trust, love, supporting each other and feeling like family.

Intimate and business relationships carry similar traits.

We may not have a 40+-year bond or even a 10-year one, but the length of the relationship isn't important. It sounds impressive but don't get caught up in the numbers. You can be with someone for 20 years in a relationship that has been dead for 18 years. You can have a healthy friendship for one year and it has changed your life for the better since day one. Don't get caught up in the length of your links. Concern yourself with the quality of the unions you have.

R&R TIME

When I moved to Cleveland after leaving TV news I met a lovely, elegant, red-haired woman named Roxanne. Someone suggested I reach out to her when I was looking to join a women's network in Northeast Ohio. I called her and we scheduled lunch.

Our luncheon ran over three hours. Some of the dinner patrons had begun to fill the now empty space. We couldn't stop talking and sharing. I trusted her enough to shed some tears over my frustrations of starting a business. I was fearful. I asked for advice and she gave it. She held my hand and told me she understood my fear. That was ten years ago.

While we hit it off instantly, it took time for our friendship to unfold. Roxanne runs a business of her own, and she sits on many boards. She was busy. I was busy. We didn't have a lot of time to nurture a relationship but gradually it came together.

I believe it came together through trust first, then humor, then compassion. Today, we take regular time for what we call R&R time: Roxanne & Raquel. Our time is our time. No cell phones or third wheels, just good food, honest conversation and lots of laughter.

I'm thrilled to have her in my front row and I'm equally thrilled to be in hers.

FILTER TOXICITY

Your relationships should be one of the top priorities in your life. How and why you spend time with the people in your life matters. It matters a lot. When your front row is working against the grain you'll know it. You will feel an emotional pull. It feels like walking in soft cement, a mixture of your desire to make the relationship work and the truth that it's not working.

Don't let your love for him or her overshadow the love you have for yourself. When toxic people come in, move out; find another space to be yourself.

Toxic people do more than drain you. They move you further away from where you want to be. They hold your journey toward Enoughness captive. It contributes to ugliness.

No matter how much you care for or love them, it will never be enough to make them whole. The energy of love is powerful but it can't transform your hope and faith. That alone will not bring them to the light if they don't have the tools to bring themselves to the light.

This was the situation of dear friends of mine, Jason and Annie. He truly loved his wife of 14 years. They had four boys and a beautiful home with all of the trappings. But Annie's head wasn't in the game. She badgered herself and at times berated Jason. She carried a lot of anger and resentment from her childhood into her marriage.

Jason encouraged marital counseling. They attended a few sessions, then Annie dropped off. Jason wanted to and tried to help his wife work through her issues but her issues were her issues. He tried to make her happy but she only found negativity in his actions. Her desire to humiliate Jason became too toxic for him. He filed for a divorce and hasn't looked back since.

Most of us have to deal with toxic people in some form or fashion, at work or even at home. We can't totally avoid them and I'm not suggesting that we stop loving them but we do have to limit our time with them. We don't want these unhappy souls in our front row.

How honest you are about seeing toxic people can alter how you see yourself and the world. We filter a lot of information without processing it. We know from my earlier section on Emotional Intelligence that processing takes being present, being fully committed to the moment. When someone is bringing negativity into your life, call it as it is, don't sugar coat it. Don't ignore it. Don't wish it away. No fairytale magic will cure a toxic friend or lover.

NATURAL INVESTMENTS

Oprah and Gayle have invested in each other. While I'm sure they weren't tracking all those late night calls or time consoling each other or fun getaway trips, I bet there is a lot of time involved. We can also put a wager on the amount of emotional investment involved in loving a friend and wanting the best for them.

To prosper in any relationship, you have to share time. You will exchange ideas, stories and dreams. This exchange is intimate and awesomely beautiful.

When people express an interest in you and share their inner desires, they are trusting you. They are investing in you. Our decision to return the investment should not feel like an obligation but a natural occurrence. It should bring pleasure.

Let your investments come naturally. Building rapport can be instant when we find people that we click with right away. Other times it will be gradual, so move when it feels right, not when you want to fulfill a fleeting need.

RELATIONSHIPS TO AVOID
Relationships that create more anxiety and anger than calm and happiness
Relationships that don't honor your growth
Relationships that talk down your magnificence
Relationships that keep you up at night with worry and sadness
Relationships that make you sick (even if the culprit provides your health insurance)
Relationships that leave bruises: physical or emotional ones
Relationships that prevent you from being all you can be
Relationship that don't easily permit you to use the tools in your Enoughness bag

ENOUGHNESS TOOL #17:
FIVE WAYS TO MAKE YOUR RELATIONSHIPS BLOOM
1. Bring Your Total Self: The entire package, everything in your Enoughness bag contributes to your total self. Healthy relationships are founded on truth and principles. Period. Make a pact to be transparent.

2. Ignite Active Listening: Listening is learning. One of the great things about listening is we can get all of the information we're seeking. We don't have to guess. The problem is when we think we know what the other person is going to say, we instantly (in our minds and sometimes out loud) finish their sentence or assume their final meaning. When we do this we stop any possibility of hearing them differently. Instead, we continue to judge and deal with them the same as before. Loved ones and admired colleagues are capable of building their own Enoughness bag. Leave room for them to grow and develop too. Become a golden listener.

3. Share Goals: Whether it be a friendship or an intimate relationship, we're more joyful people when we're working toward a goal. It gives us something to look forward to and celebrate together. You can develop goal lines with your friends just as you can with your life partner. Let your goal list be the adhesive for sharing accomplishments and dreams with each other.

4. Create Healthy Boundaries: Don't make people guess when they're crossing the lines. Tell them. Don't wait for an argument to set someone straight. Share your limits in a loving conversation. Creating harmony in relationships is crucial. Setting boundaries will support conformity. It's your job to let people know where you stand.

5. Embrace Disagreements: Process disagreements the same way you would process a promotion; with grace and grit. Highlight what the two of you are doing right and where you want to go from here. Spend less time discussing the hiccup but be certain to clean it up and restore integrity if needed. Lingering in our darker moments isn't healthy and doesn't support our expedition to wholeness.

Time doesn't erase old wounds. You do.

SELF FORGIVENESS

Forgiveness isn't an eraser. It doesn't eliminate the act. It doesn't delete the wrong or strip away the pain. It doesn't have a safety net or magic potion.

But it is extremely freeing. It loosens us from the grip of mean-spiritedness. What it does is unload the hardness and hatred toward the act and the perpetrator.

It's easy to say that we should forgive others and ourselves. It's easy to repeat the phrase "Get over it already" or "Just let it go." Getting over it doesn't really happen until we get up close and personal with the situation. Getting over it can not possibly happen until we process the emotions and put them into proper perspective.

Forgiveness is less about the other people involved and more about you. But what happens when it's you that you need to forgive? What if you need to release yourself from the agony perpetuated by your own hand? How do you work on pardoning yourself for screwing up?

100 PAPER CUTS

I do understand, stuff happens. We lose control. We make mistakes. Life can be like a shredder, ripping you in several directions, leaving you limp and lifeless. Tough things produce tough times. This is how it goes for everyone. We all take our turn. The difference is how we make our way back to a solid sense of self.

When your spirit has been crushed and your soul wounded, you ebb and flow in life. When you don't nurse yourself back to a state of completeness or wholeness, the smallest missteps can feel monumental. They can feel like one hundred paper cuts on one finger.

Stop. This pain can be avoided.

Forgiving yourself is how you mend the divide within. It's how you place a calm lid on a fire that's been brewing over time. Self forgiveness marries well with the wholeness we all want and deserve.

EXTEND THE INVITATION

There is good news and more good news. First, nothing is lost here. It might be tucked away but you can reclaim it. The other good news is that self forgiveness is closer than you think. You only have to invite it in.

Janice was on a fast track to success working in a small but fast-growing marketing firm. She was up for a promotion but her boss asked her to "hang tight" as they waited for a few clients to make substantial payments on their accounts.

In the meantime Janice was asked to take on more work which required working overtime. She was promised a big payday and promotion as soon as more funds rolled in. In the meantime a lot of work needed to be done.

A single mother of three, Janice was excited about the promotion and had known her boss for several years. She trusted her boss and believed in her mission. Even though two employees warned Janice about their boss's tendency to over-promise and under-deliver, Janice ignored their warnings. She chalked it up to office gossip and envy.

A month turned into six months and then a year. Janice's boss kept giving the same updates. "It's taking more time than we thought, our clients are delivering very soon."

A total of 17 months passed and Janice was still in the same predicament but now she had racked up hours of work that took time away from family and other obligations. When it finally clicked that she was being misled, Janice got angry. She was angry with her boss but for some reason she was more angry at herself.

Janice cursed herself for being "stupid" and wondered, "Why didn't I see that coming?" She was upset over the lost time and the money that she knew she would never see. She badgered herself. Shame and humiliation consumed her. She knew she had been taken advantage of. People tried to warn her but she kept the faith.

PUMP THE BRAKES

Janice did a dangerous thing. She connected this situation to all the other mistakes she made in the past. She grouped all the times she chose kindness over sensible thinking. She traveled down a rabbit hole. That's how we become stuck and distressed.

With all the stuff coming at you, you want your Enoughness bag to glide across those rough patches in the pavement. Looping the present moment to past baggage will have you pumping the brakes at each step.

Emotional bondage to past errors should be broken and separated from current situations. The two really have nothing to do with each other except for the fact that you are repeating a cycle. Don't drag the baggage into the now. Interrupt the cycle. Find out what is within you that gives you permission to tear yourself down during personal challenges. What makes it OK? Fix how you feel about it and yourself.

Janice had to learn to heal. She had to forgive herself.

Janice is no different from any of us. She is no different from me. I had to learn how to heal from mistakes. I had to learn how to accept regret. I want it to teach me, not rule me. I had to learn to forgive myself for breaking that promise to my younger self, for losing my footing and letting things go awry.

Not only did I beat myself up for what happened, I was angry for not having a plan in place. I had those "How can you be so stupid?" moments which is nothing short of tormenting the soul.

A CRACK IN YOUR ARMOR

As is common with many of us, something was lacking in Janice. She had given herself permission to be in these predicaments. This wasn't the first time she felt like a doormat.

My advice to Janice was the same advice I gave myself; listen to what life is telling you, learn the lesson and have a plan in place. All of those things may not prevent a devastating event from occurring but they will help you manage it in a more effective way that protects your soul.

It is so important that we do the homework and get the lesson. If we don't we will be confronted with similar situations that will prompt repeat behavior. Life keeps reminding us of the lessons we have to learn until we actually learn them. I suggested to Janice that she not hold her tongue or retreat to her corner. Stand up, take it straight, no chaser. Face it. Stick to your new way of solving issues.

We can't become whole again without understanding where we tucked parts of ourselves. Janice had to do that. You have to do that. I have to do that.

You were born with everything you need. Then, you were stripped of it or maybe you gave it away. Maybe in itty bitty pieces or chunks at a time. We break the most sacred of links; a connection to our authentic selves. Every single person I know has more than one of these cracks. We all have to do some mending as we work our way back to being whole and complete.

By the way, that popular line in the movie Jerry Maguire when Tom Cruise's character says to his love interest, "You complete me" is only true in the movies. No one can complete you but you. The onus rests solely on you.

ENOUGHNESS TOOL #18:
EIGHT STEPS TO PRACTICE SELF FORGIVENESS

Linking back up with yourself can start today with big action in the following small steps:

1. Transform Sour Emotions: If you are holding a grudge or ill feelings for others or yourself, work through forgiveness by softening your heart each day. Speak kindly and softly about the person who played a role in your separation from self. Being angry is permissible but give yourself a timeline for this, like seven minutes. Bounce kindness and compassion in for the remaining time. Use kind words to elevate your self-awareness and maturity. Be gentle with yourself.

2. Find Gratitude: Focus on what you have now instead of past loss and grief. Make it an absolute rule to never use your misfortune from the past as an excuse for not counting the blessings in the present. Find gratitude every day. It will soften your heart and your face. When I remember to give thanks for clean running water, suddenly I'm reminded of the many people who don't have clean running water. The same with shelter and food and even love. A lot of people don't have those things but if you do, expressing thanks is the right thing to do.

3. Sprint to Forgiveness: Time doesn't heal old wounds. You heal them. You make an agreement with yourself to stop carrying resentment and replace it with resiliency. Only you can do this. Time has nothing to do with erasing pain. Drop the idea that forgiveness takes time, and instead sprint toward it. Your inability to let things go is only hurting you. You are prolonging your own suffering. Work quickly to loosen the grip it has on you. The sooner you can do this the sooner you will meet the bright, brilliant life that awaits you.

4. Walk it Out: Find a wide, open space in nature and dive into it. When you take a walk on the beach, become one with it. When you walk through the forest, be with it. Nature is perfection. It teaches us patience and reminds us to slow down and let things take their course. Walking through some of life's most beautiful places brings clarity and peace.

5. Send Love: In the book Eat, Pray, Love, Elizabeth Gilbert suggests that we meditate on sending warm thoughts to people we may have hurt. Being still and sending love energy from your heart removes those tarnished feelings. Putting good vibes out into the universe creates more positive energy. Each time a negative thought arises, counter it with love energy. Keep doing it until the foulness dissipates.

6. Seek the Best: Being hopeful wins the battle over hurt and pain. Some days, when the tides seem to be rolling in faster than you can stand, try this simple wish or prayer: May the best thing that can happen, happen. Some things are out of your control, there is a larger power at work here that is all knowing and all encompassing.

7. Tell a Story: Start journaling. Write about what happened and all the feelings you associate with the experience. Then be sure your outcome tells a story with a positive, heroic outcome. Write more than a happy ending, write an ending that is impactful, one that you would want to read to every hopeful little girl and boy in the world. Build a system through daily entries and write with intention. The intention is to heal and grow.

8. Put On Your Cape: You were born into the world with everything you needed. You were covered when you arrived. You were caped. You've always had a cape. You decided the color and type of material, and embellished it with the gems you've collected through life. Have fun with it. Make it match your personality.

See the cape travel with you all through your formative and adolescent years. See your cape flying behind you down Harker Hill and getting a little tousled during the skid in the gravel. Follow your power cape through your young adult years right up to where you are today. Your cape is your protection from all the outside stuff. It is your heroine coat. Your bravery and boldness keep it intact. Leave space for it in your Enoughness bag. Take it out each time you need to work through when people wrong you or when you wrong yourself. Remember where you come from: Pure, essential goodness. Like your cape flying in the wind, so do bad feelings. Let them go.

BONUS ENOUGHNESS

Thrill Seeker? Start a Movement. Gatherer?
Bring Others to the Movement. Silent Supporter? Speak Up.

WOMEN HELPING WOMEN

No one gets to the top alone. You need help. You need someone to open the door for you and at times, someone to push you through the foyer. I added this bonus section because we need each other to move the needle. Building a strong sisterhood can make all the difference. Finding the right support is not easy for many women. They deal with disgruntled females who come with an ulterior motive or just flat out don't want to help other women soar.

This attitude is problematic for many reasons, but mainly because it slows our progress toward equality. It slows our climb to the top and for real change.

Starting a new business in a new city brings its own stress. No matter how determined I felt, there were roadblocks on nearly every corner. I did all the right things, attended networking and fundraising events, volunteered for various organizations, set up face-to-face meetings but I was still being met with one bad girl after another.

Some of the women had faulty attitudes and poor communication skills. Their disingenuousness was very unappealing. They seemed to have somehow ended up on a pedestal either by their own doing or by their groupies.

"GOOGLE ME"

One time, I met a woman of influence at a conference in Cleveland. I explained that I was writing a weekly newspaper column and would like to run a few ideas by her. I asked for her business card.

She responded, "Oh, just Google me." While Google can help us with many things, getting her email address wasn't one of them. Her unprofessionalism wasn't only unpleasant but left a blemish on her personal brand.

In another bad girl example, I asked a woman to speak at my Woman of Power Conference. For some unknown reason she was very interested in the amount of money I was making. When I told her it was none of her business she distanced herself from the project and stopped returning calls. I removed her from the agenda. She blocked me on Twitter. I know, very mature.

Another woman actually invited me to dinner and inquired about my work and strategy. She posed as a friend. The next year she copied one of my projects, followed up with most of my contacts and stamped her name on it. At least she paid for dinner which by the way was not a tasty meal.

Women with this lazy disposition are waiting around an entirely different baggage claim area where luggage rolls out battered and ripped. Things are always missing from their Enoughness bags because their perspective is based on scarcity. Lack follows people with closed hearts and closed minds. They always blame others for messing up that bag.

Women who fail to help other women have created a monumental wall of malice that adds more division to an already divisive world. We won't mend that brokenness overnight but we can chip away at some of what is causing our unity to erode. Together, we can ignite a transformational healing within ourselves and shoot down the madness that mutilates the esteem of another woman.

WOMEN WHO GO THE DISTANCE

Even though some sisters are closed to the idea of helping other women thrive, I still have my eye on the prize and I see this working out for all of us. On the flip side I have had some very incredible, sensational women open doors for me. My life has been greatly enriched by several outstanding women who believe in the notion of carrying as you climb.

Their sponsorship, mentorship and friendship has sparked real change. This group opened doors without reservation, without a mention of a returned favor. For these women, I kiss their ring. Their belief in women helping women has been a catalyst for bigger and better things. My journey has expanded because of their emotional and spiritual contributions.

I'm in awe of how far I've come because of these women.

Growing up in a small midwestern town meant life was routine. One of those routines was traveling the same routes every day, absorbing the same sights. There was a billboard promoting cigarettes and I remember a tall, slender woman modeling in the photo. What stood out more to me was the slogan: "You've come a long way, baby."

As a kid, I had no idea how the slogan connected to cigarettes. While the puff sticks never made their way to my lips, that catchphrase did. It lingered in the background of my life. Even today, it reappears during moments of personal reflection and determination. It's there when I think about the trajectory of my life and the people around me. I've come a long way. I know many women who have stood the test of time. Their travel bags have weathered many storms. Many of us wrote our own rules and changed the game. We are mythbusters and fairness chasers. So many of us have gone against the grain.

The strides we made as women are nothing short of significant and gutsy. We have to pick up the pace and I am excited and inspired by our next move.

PAVE THE WAY

CEO of KeyCorp Beth Mooney says she thinks about the women who will someday follow in her footsteps. The work she does now is intentional for other women. In a Fortune.com interview, Mooney told Susie Gharib that she felt obligated to pave the way. "Women were looking to me to do this well, not just in the bank but across the country." The leader of KeyBank said this is a daily effort. "Every day I get up to do this job with an extra special sense of doing it well because

I think it will create the path for others to follow. I hope my legacy is that others will follow and that I made it easier for young women to aspire to this kind of job and for others to see women in this kind of role."

NEW MOTIVATION

Right now there is a new energy surging. This book was published during the Donald Trump era, a challenging time for America: In 2017 more sexual harassment cases hit mainstream media, causing some very popular, well established men to face their fate. Supporters of Trump have been pitted against non-supporters. Racism and sexism have been routinely discussed in the media.

With all of this, in March of 2017 women all over the country put a plan into action and marched for racial equality, freedom of religion, LGBTQ rights, immigration reform, healthcare reform, reproductive rights and workers' rights. The Women's March on Washington reportedly had over 5 million demonstrators spill into the streets of Philadelphia PA, Seattle WA, Washington D.C. and other cities. I witnessed unity, a collective consciousness. Although these controversial issues are unresolved, they are far from dead. Millions of women have aligned with their values and passion. They have kept things alive. We've come a long way, baby.

With this movement of togetherness, I feel a responsibility to pull my sisters into a huddle to contemplate how to continue the momentum. How can we build on not only the Women's March in Washington of 2017 but the Women's Suffrage Movement of 1848 and every other bold movement between the two?

ACTIVATE POWER!

To do it, you and I must activate our woman power. Each of us has been helped along the way. On their shoulders we stand. Paying it forward is a natural progression in life. As you move forward, carry another woman with you. Challenge others to do the same.

Finding a female in your inner circle with a similar mindset might be difficult. Instead, you might find a purse full of judgment, a ring of jealousy and a compact of comparison. For some it seems the more women they try to pull together, the more the fundamental purpose dissolves into chaos. Don't try to change these women. We don't have the bandwidth or the time. We can still help them by helping others.

The goal isn't to hurt hurting women but by sharpening our Enoughness and working for change, we make the world better for everyone. When we plant a seed to do good by others, we're doing good by all, even people with sour attitudes.

As you move into the idea of empowering yourself and others, think on a global scale and include everyone, even the woman who blocks you on Twitter or the one who wants you to Google her.

BONUS ENOUGHNESS TOOL:
BUILD YOUR SISTERHOOD

1. Start a Movement: Before my conference became a conference, it was a small three-hour seminar at a motel in Belleville, Ohio. Over 20 women attended and it started a conversation. You can do it with three women or 300.

2. Be Level Headed: Build a brain trust of like-minded women around you. Find women who both agree and strike a chord on issues pertinent to you. To achieve true progress, you need to hear both sides of the issue. Approach your group with a cool head even if a fire burns in your belly. People can hear you better when you speak from intellect over emotion.

3. Integrate: Many women's groups are doing good work. They are collaborating and calling out the culprits. Share your voice with those who are making a difference. We didn't come all this way with one woman. Many have had to take a seat at the table. Take your seat at the table. Engage with other agents of change. Also bring men into the conversation. I have had enormous support from some male colleagues. Men manage differently. Many of them are cheering for women. Find the good ones and ask for input.

4. Be Results Driven: Don't be all about the talk. We've done a lot of conversing about great topics but action is what we all need now. After group discussions, outline the problems in your organization. Initiate the next step. Seek solutions. Help lead your group to solving them. Work together to repair any damage and prepare for the next steps.

Who Taught You To Fly? Pass On
The Lessons, Combined With
New Wisdom. Give Them Away.

Stay curious.

RESOURCES

Emotional Intelligence Article
Internet Resource: https://hbr.org/2017/02/emotional-intelligence-has-12-elements-which-do-you-need-to-work-on

Clear Closet:
Kondo, Marie, "The Life-Changing Magic of Tidying Up: the Japanese art of decluttering and organizing," Ten Speed Press, New York, 2014

Forgiveness:
Gilbert, Elizabeth, "Eat, Pray, Love", Riverhead Books, New York, 2007

Joyful Living:
Internet resource for laughing: https://www.psychologytoday.com/blog/the-possibility-paradigm/201106/youre-not-laughing-enough-and-thats-no-joke

Women Helping Women:
Internet Resource: Beth Mooney
http://fortune.com/video/2018/01/10/keycorp-ceo-never-say-no-to-a-challenge/

Additional Resources: Blackburn, Elizabeth and Epel, Elissa, "The Telomere Effect," New York, Grand Central Publishing, 2017
Chopra, Deepak, M.D, "Ageless Mind, Timeless Body," United States: Three Rivers Press, 1993

Collins, Jim, "Good to Great," New York, HarperCollins Publishing Inc., 2001

Hay, Louise, "You Can Heal Your Life," California: Hay House, 1999

Schucman, Helen, "A Course in Miracles," New York, Viking: The Foundation of Peace, 1976

Internet Resource: Swami Sivananda, "Law of Retribution," The Divine Life Society, 2011 http://sivanandaonline.org/public_html/?cmd=display-section&section_id=1160

PLUG-IN RESOURCES
TO HELP YOU THRIVE

DEAR READERS,

The following section is intended to become your partner in honing your Enoughness. While building your career or business you need to plug in to positive outlets every day. Having an array of positive notes coming through your inbox and social feeds can do more than uplift your mood; it can inspire creativity and promote wellness.

On the following pages, you'll find a variety of resources that will support your journey to success if you allow it. Take some time to review them and take what you need to propel yourself forward.

Websites to Inspire You

Daily Good
News that inspires.
dailygood.org

Global Positive News Network
Dedicated to helping you exorcise the negative influences from your life so you can enjoy each day to its fullest.
globalpositivenewsnetwork.com

Good News Network
A clearinghouse for the gathering and dissemination of positive news stories from around the globe.
goodnewsnetwork.org

Hooplaha
Only good news.
hooplaha.com

Optimist World
Celebrates the best in life and is inspired by the joy around us.
optimistworld.com

Positive News
Positive News promises good journalism about good things.
positive.news

Simple Most
Simple Most's mission is to provide women with news that can impact their lives, along with ideas and tips to help make things just a little easier.
simplemost.com

Sunny Skyz

Sunny Skyz's slogan is: Positive, upbeat media. Live. Laugh. Love.

sunnyskyz.com

Today Good News

Their Good News is inspirational, uplifting and happy news, photos, videos and more.

today.com/news/good-news

Conferences to Empower You

Catalyst
An international event that addresses topics vital to women in the workplace.
New York, New York and other locations
catalyst.org/catalyst-awards-conference

Diversity Woman
A leadership empowerment event for women who mean business.
Magazine & Conference
National Harbor, MD
diversitywoman.com

Financial Women's Association
The association has a mission of advancing women.
Toronto and Vancouver, Canada
member.fwa.org

Forbes Women's Summit
Brings the world's most influential leaders, policy-makers, entrepreneurs and artists together to address today's critical issues and discover innovative solutions.
New York, New York
forbes.com/forbes-live/event/womens-summit

Pennsylvania Conference for Women
The mission of the conference is to promote, communicate and amplify the influence of women in the workplace and beyond.
paconferenceforwomen.org

Professional Business Women of California (PBWC) Conference
A non-profit organization promoting equality and career momentum through events, webinars and a network of leading business professionals.
San Francisco, CA
pbwcconference.org

Simmons Leadership Conference
The preeminent authority on women's leadership.
Boston, MA
simmons.edu/leadership

Texas Conference for Women
The state's premier educational and networking event for women.
Austin, TX
txconferenceforwomen.org

Women for Economic and Leadership Development (WELD)
WELD provides programs and events for women seeking leadership development opportunities at all levels of their organizations and for women business owners. Find a chapter near you.
weldusa.org

**Woman of Power Conference (WoPC),
a Raquel Eatmon Leadership Forum**
WoPC is the Midwest's premier leadership and social change conference for achieving women in industry, government, academia, non-profit and entrepreneurs.
Cleveland, OH
TheWoPC.com

Women in the World Summit
The premier showcase for women of impact and for the men who champion them.
New York, New York
womenintheworld.com/events/the-women-in-the-world-summit

Newsletters and Podcasts to Inform You

INFLUENTIAL WEBSITES

ProjectHeard.com
A leadership forum showcasing 50 bloggers on topics in Leadership, Entrepreneurship, Lifestyle and Wellness.
projectheard.com

Success
Personal and professional development news for busy people who aim to develop practices and philosophies to live powerful and extraordinary lives.
success.com

Thrive Global
Offers sustainable science-based solutions to enhance well-being, performance, and purpose and create a healthier relationship with technology.
thriveglobal.com

Women of the World
A non-profit organization that helps refugee women to achieve self-reliance and economic success in any stage of resettlement.
womenofworld.org

World Wide Women
A resource platform for women who want trusted information. Their mission is to connect women and girls around the world with valuable organizations, programs, and services that have the potential to positively impact their lives. A unique feature is their Buy FromWomen directory to purchase goods and services from women-owned businesses.
worldwidewomen.co

INFLUENTIAL PODCASTS

Appearance Matters: The Podcast!
From the Centre of Appearance Research investigating body image and appearance psychology research.
soundcloud.com/appearance-matters

Kate's Take Podcast
Behind the Scenes of a 7-Figure Business
www.eofire.com/audio-blog

The Lively Show with Jess Lively
Covers a variety of topics from blogging to business, wellness and food.
jesslively.com/livelyshow

Recode Decode hosted by Kara Swisher
News on tech and interviews with business leaders and other personalities.
recode.net/recode-decode-podcast-kara-swisher

What Works Podcast hosted by Tara Gentile
What really works to run, manage and grow small businesses today.
cocommercial.co/whatworks/

Movements to Support

Girls Not Brides
A global partnership of more than 650 civil society organizations from nearly 100 countries committed to ending child marriage and enabling girls to fulfill their potential.
girlsnotbrides.org

Girls on the Run
Empowers young girls to take charge of their lives and blossom into their full potential. Classes meet twice a week and encourage girls to express themselves through movement.
girlsontherun.org

Girls Who Code
An organization working to close the gender gap in technology by helping girls become better equipped with the tools they need to innovate and create change.
girlswhocode.com

Keep Abreast Foundation
Provides young people with breast cancer education and support.
keep-a-breast.org

Sewing Hope
A foundation led by Sister Rosemary's charge to help human trafficking survivors become self-sufficient and empowered through designing pop-tab handbags to support their families. The initiative provides jobs and hope to many women in Uganda and South Sudan.
sewinghope.com

She Should Run
A national network changing culture to inspire more women and girls to run for office.
sheshouldrun.org

Sheppard's Hands

Offers long-term housing solely to female veterans and ensures that the women it serves have access to medical care and counseling, job training, help with computer skills, financial planning and other assistance.
sheppardshands.org

Women on Wings

Aims to create one million jobs for women in rural India. A job means an income, economic autonomy and an escape from the cycle of poverty. Research shows that women spend their income on their families. Children can go to school, which increases their chances of a better future.
womenonwings.com

Women for Women International

Takes a comprehensive approach to social and economic empowerment of marginalized women and help women apply their strength to overcome challenges.
womenforwomen.org

YWCA Greater Cleveland NIA program

Nurturing Independence & Aspirations (NIA) program is a Trauma-Informed System of Care model focused on permanence, education, employment, housing, physical and mental health, and personal and community engagement for youth 18-24 years of age transition from failing systems including foster care.
ywcaofcleveland.org

LEADERSHIP LABS AND COURSES TO EDUCATE YOU

CASE WESTERN RESERVE UNIVERSITY

Leadership Lab for Women in Manufacturing

An in-depth learning experience providing leadership development education and training to women in mid- to high-level management roles in manufacturing careers.

Weatherhead School of Management, Case Western Reserve University
womeninmanufacturing.org/leadership-lab

Leadership Lab for Women in STEM

A flexible, blended experience of in-person and online learning to help develop women's careers and leadership in science, technology, engineering, and mathematics (STEM) workplaces.

Weatherhead School of Management, Case Western Reserve University
weatherhead.case.edu/executive-education/programs/women-in-stem

Women in Leadership Certificate

A series of four one-day educational seminars enabling women to develop leadership skills.

Weatherhead School of Management, Case Western Reserve University
weatherhead.case.edu/executive-education/certificates/women-in-leadership

Free Massive Open Online Course (MOOC)

Women in Leadership: Inspiring Positive Change!

Flexible, online learning program aimed at inspiring and empowering women and men around the world to engage in purposeful career development and take on leadership for important causes, to lead change with more conviction and confidence, and to improve our workplaces and communities for all. Taught by Professor Diana Bilimoria of Case Western Reserve University.

www.coursera.org/learn/women-in-leadership

Cornell University Online
E-Cornell online courses will help you gain experience in executive leadership and teach you how to successfully spearhead a team. You will gain in-depth instruction in change management, negotiation, cultivating creativity, and making critical, time-sensitive decisions. This certificate is ideal for professionals looking for an executive leadership development program to improve their leadership skills and move their careers to a higher level.
onlinelearning.cornell.edu/executive-leadership

Harvard Leadership Courses
Whether you are your own CEO or working at a for-profit or non-profit organization, develop your leadership and strategic management skills through learning content such as: Developing myself, managing evidence, driving change and more.
online-learning.harvard.edu/leadership

MIT Open Course Ware — Sloan School of Management
A world-class business school long renowned for thought leadership and the ability to successfully partner theory and practice. Visit the website for a list of current courses.
ocw.mit.edu/courses/sloan-school-of-management

HELPLINES TO SUPPORT YOU

Disaster Distress Helpline
1-800-985-5990

Equal Employment Opportunity Commission
1-800-669-4000

Gift from Within
(Not a hotline. A helpful link for survivors of trauma and victimization.)
1-207-236-8858

National Alliance on Mental Illness
1-800-950-6264

National Coalition of Anti-Violence Programs
National Advocacy for Local LGBT Communities
1-212-714-1141

National Domestic Violence Hotline
1-800-799-7233 or 1-800-787-3224 (TTY)

National Sexual Assault Hotline
1-800-656-4673

National Suicide Prevention Lifeline
1-800-273-TALK (8255)
1-888-628-9454 (Spanish)
1-800-799-4889 (TTY)

The Trevor Project
Crisis & Suicide Prevention Lifeline for LGBTQ Youth
1-866-488-7386

WAGE Job Survival Hotline
Provides information on sexual harassment, family leave, pregnancy discrimination and other employment issues.
1-800-522-0925

Questioning our Enoughness
is absurd because being enough,
being whole is our birthright.

Beyond Enough
How to Lead with Your Whole Self
Published by: Rising Media LLC, Cleveland, Ohio
Copyright 2018 by Raquel Eatmon

The Library of Congress has catalogued as follows:
ISBN: 978-0-692-09404-4
First American Paperback Edition

Printed in United States of America

Original Book Cover design by Dana Anderson, The Beehive Studio, LLC.
Copies can be ordered at: www.RaquelEatmon.com

About the Author

Raquel Eatmon is the CEO of Rising Media LLC. She is a recognized national speaker on women's leadership, author of two books, and founder of the Woman of Power Conference and ProjectHeard.com online women's forum. She is a former television news reporter / anchor. She was the voice behind the 10-year running newspaper column Be Inspired with Raquel with Gannett. She is a mentor and advocate for social change.

Ready to continue the conversation? Share your #BeyondEnough experience. Connect with Raquel at RaquelEatmon.com and on Twitter, LinkedIn, FaceBook and Instagram: @RaquelEatmon

Thank you!

Made in the USA
Columbia, SC
19 January 2023

10732316R00104